Birds of Prey

Birds
of Prey

Michael Everett

G.P. PUTNAM'S SONS · NEW YORK

© Orbis Publishing Limited, London
SBN: 399–11675–3
Library of Congress Catalog Card Number: 75–18596
Printed in Italy by IGDA, Novara

Frontispiece: White-bellied Sea Eagle about to catch a fish
(Hans and Judy Beste: Ardea Photographics)
Endpapers: Augur Buzzard (Jane Burton: Bruce Coleman)

Contents

Acknowledgements

KEY: A above; B below; L left; R right
We are most grateful to the following for permission to reproduce the photographs on the following pages: Front cover Moira Borland/Bruce Coleman; Back cover Hans and Judy Beste/Ardea Photographics, London; Back flap Bryan Sage/Ardea; Front flap R. M. Bloomfield/Ardea; Endpapers Jane Burton/Bruce Coleman; Frontispiece Hans and Judy Beste/Ardea; 8 John Pearson/Bruce Coleman; 10 Eric Hosking; 11 Jane Burton/Bruce Coleman; 12 Peter Green/Ardea; 14 James Simon/Bruce Coleman; 15A Clem Haagner/Ardea; 15B Peter Steyn/Ardea; 16 Kenneth Fink/Ardea; 18A Joe Van Wormer/Bruce Coleman; 18B Adrian Warren/Ardea; 19A Hans and Judy Beste/Ardea; 19B L. R. Dawson/Bruce Coleman; 20 Ardea Photographics, London; 21 Hans Reinhard/Bruce Coleman; 22A Eric Hosking; 22BL M. D. England/Ardea; 22BR Eric Hosking; 23 Charlie Ott/Bruce Coleman; 24 P. Blasdale/Ardea; 26 John Pearson/Bruce Coleman; 27A John Wightman/Ardea; 27B John Pearson/Bruce Coleman; 28AL Ardea Photographics, London; 28AR Clem Haagner/Ardea; 28B Peter Steyn/Ardea; 29L Leslie H. Brown/Ardea; 29R Richard Waller/Ardea; 30 Gary Jones/Ardea; 31 Hans Reinhard/Bruce Coleman; 32 Jane Burton/Bruce Coleman; 33BL Alan Weaving/Ardea; 33AR, 33BR Francisco Erize/Bruce Coleman; 34 Kenneth Fink/Ardea; 35 M. D. England/Ardea; 36L A. J. Deane/Bruce Coleman; 36R Clem Haagner/Ardea; 37 Eric Hosking; 38 Peter Steyn/Ardea; 39 Kenneth Fink/Ardea; 40AL J. L. Mason/Ardea; 40BL Clem Haagner/Ardea; 40R M. D. England/Ardea; 41AR John Wightman/Ardea; 41BR H. Rivarola/Bruce Coleman; 42 Bruce Coleman; 44L Eric Hosking; 44R Kenneth Fink/Ardea; 45 Eric Hosking; 46A Peter Steyn/Ardea; 46B Leslie H. Brown/Ardea; 47 E. McNamara/Ardea; 49 E. Breeze Jones/Bruce Coleman; 50 Alan Weaving/Ardea; 51A Helmut Albrecht/Bruce Coleman; 51B Bruce Coleman; 52L, 52R Christopher Mylne; 53 Eric Hosking; 54 H. M. Barnfather/Bruce Coleman; 56 R. Balharry; 58 S. Roberts/Ardea; 59 G. D. Plage/Survival Anglia Ltd.; 60A Eric Hosking; 60B R. J. C. Blewitt/Ardea; 61A J. B. and S. Bottomley/Ardea; 61B R. J. C. Blewitt/Ardea; 63 A. Fatras/Jacana; 64 Jane Burton/Bruce Coleman; 65 Falconry Centre, Newent, Glos., England; 66 Charlie Ott/Bruce Coleman; 67 Hans and Judy Beste/Ardea; 68 G. D. Plage/Bruce Coleman; 69 M. D. England/Ardea; 70 Peter Steyn/Ardea; 71A A. J. Deane/Bruce Coleman; 71B John Pearson/Bruce Coleman; 72 Rod Borland/Bruce Coleman; 74 Hans and Judy Beste/Ardea; 75 Joseph Van Wormer/Bruce Coleman; 76 Peter Steyn/Ardea; 78 Don MacCaskill/A.F.A. Ltd.; 79 Bruce Coleman; 80 Lee Lyon/Bruce Coleman; 81 R. M. Bloomfield/Ardea; 83 D. V. Nostrand/Frank W. Lane; 84 Leonard Lee Rue III/Bruce Coleman; 85 Peter Steyn/Ardea; 86A, 86B Eric Hosking; 87 Hans and Judy Beste/Ardea; 88 Eric Hosking; 90A Christopher Mylne/Ardea; 90B Christopher Mylne; 91 Geoffrey Kinns; 92 Graham Pizzey/Bruce Coleman; 93 Peter Steyn/Ardea; 94 Christopher Mylne; 97 R. Balharry; 98 Graham Pizzey/Bruce Coleman; 99A P. Morris/Ardea; 99B James Simon/Bruce Coleman; 101L J. A. Bailey/Ardea; 101R Bryan Sage/Ardea; 102 Bruce Coleman; 104 Kenneth Fink/Ardea; 106 R.S.P.B.; 107 C. Rabanit/Jacana; 108L John Wightman/Ardea; 108R, 109 Frank S. Todd, Corporate Curator of Birds, Sea World; 110A S. Roberts/Ardea; 110B R.S.P.B.; 111A R.S.P.B./Intertech Ltd.; 111B Peter Robinson/R.S.P.B.; 112 Survival Anglia Ltd.; 113A Peter Alden/Ardea; 113B Eric Hosking; 114 R. Balharry; 115 Christopher Mylne/Ardea; 116 R. T. Smith/Ardea; 117 R.S.P.B.; 118L, 118R Falconry Centre, Newent, Glos., England; 119 Eric Hosking; 120 G. D. Plage/Bruce Coleman. The Species List on pages 122–125, is taken from *Eagles, Hawks and Falcons of the World* by Leslie Brown and Dean Amadon (Country Life Books, 1968) and appears by permission of The Hamlyn Group.

Foreword

by PETER CONDER, *Director of the Royal Society for the Protection of Birds*

It is essential today that we develop greater understanding of birds of prey. Because they kill other creatures, the more sentimental among us tend to think that these birds are somehow unpleasant or cruel, and ignore the robin's predation on worms. In contrast, other people tend to think of themselves as the only creatures with a right to kill – indiscriminately shooting or trapping hawks or falcons without understanding their role in the natural environment.

Nowadays we try to see nature as a community of living and non-living things. We see the community as having structure, as a forest has structure, and that it also has energy which is transferred from one creature to another. Energy is derived first from the chemicals in the soil which are acted upon by sun and rain. It is taken up by plants in a form that some insects, mammals and birds can consume. In their turn, these creatures are consumed by larger animals, with predators such as the birds of prey at the end of the web. When they die, they are consumed by microbes and the energy contained in their bodies is returned to the soil. Nature is not complete without the animals which prey on and eat flesh.

Birds of prey are among the most skilled and spectacular of all birds in their hunting methods – every aspect of their lives is adapted to the seasonal and geographical abundance of food. Their livelihood depends on the ability to kill and the abundance of their prey. Recently, the fortunes of birds of prey throughout the world have suffered because man has changed their habitats, misused lethal chemicals and increasingly developed an antipathy for them in the mistaken belief that they cause substantial damage to livestock. Their numbers have declined so much that one wonders if some of the eagles and vultures are not as doomed as the dinosaur. We need a far greater understanding of them, and I believe that Michael Everett's book has a chance of helping us in this.

Michael Everett's sympathy, understanding and deep knowledge of birds of prey are apparent in his book. He writes simply and authoritatively, often describing his personal experiences of them. I like his book for he is a true lover of birds of prey, not a 'grasper' who wants to have the bird on his fist, or in a bird garden. He likes them where they should be – wild and free.

Introduction

Birds of prey have always held a deeply-rooted fascination for man. He has worshipped them and used them as symbols of his highest aspirations – or he has found them repulsive and slaughtered them quite ruthlessly. In whatever way he has regarded them, it has seldom been with indifference.

In spite of all the benevolent or hostile feelings which they elicit, relatively little is known about many birds of prey, and even the most familiar are the objects of totally fanciful stories. To many who rear livestock or gamebirds, birds of prey are simply vermin to be controlled, while to the average layman they are cruel and merciless killers. Studies suggest, however, that birds of prey are not normally hostile to man's interests, and although in certain circumstances a few may cause damage, a fair number are distinctly beneficial.

Birds of prey are those birds which belong to the Order Falconiformes. This includes such birds as falcons, hawks, harriers, kites, eagles, vultures and buzzards. All of them kill other creatures or feed on their dead carcasses. For zoological reasons other bird species, such as owls, which also take live prey, are not included in this Order.

The many misconceptions which have prevailed concerning the role of birds of prey in nature or indeed of any predatory animal arise through a lack of knowledge of their life histories and their relationships with other living creatures. In the last three decades in particular, ornithologists have made detailed studies of many species – especially in Europe, North America and Africa – which have contributed greatly to our understanding of this fascinating

Left : Indian White-backed Vulture coming in to land – to some, a magnificent bird ; to others, quite repulsive

9

group of birds. The ornithologists, however, would be the first to admit that we have only seen the tip of the iceberg. Equally, while considerable progress has been made in conveying this knowledge to the non-specialist, a great deal of research into the Order Falconiformes is still needed.

Birds of prey have an obvious attraction for the naturalist, whether he is a weekend bird-watcher or an ornithologist engaged on research, but in recent years they have been the objects of increasing interest and concern to a relatively new group: the nature conservationists. Some species have long been at risk due to persecution in one form or another, while others are so locally distributed or are so highly specialized that the slightest disturbance to their way of life could endanger them. The threats to some species posed by collectors and trophy-hunters are both real and long-standing. More recently, however, the indirect dangers arising from many of man's activities have gained a new and sinister significance. Increasing urbanization and industrialization, the drainage of more and more wetlands, the destruction of woodlands (and, conversely, wide-scale afforestation) and rapidly changing methods of agriculture lead to loss of

habitat, increasing human pressures on the environment and diverse forms of pollution. In many regions the pressures on wildlife have become critical and, because they occupy a key position in the balance of nature, many birds of prey are endangered as they never were before.

Thus the need to know more about them ceases to be purely a matter of scientific curiosity and assumes a greater urgency; for without a wide understanding of these creatures and their ecology our efforts to conserve them will be to little avail, and few would deny that they are worthy of preservation, either on scientific, moral or aesthetic grounds.

This book outlines the parlous position of many birds of prey today, and, in examining the reasons, considers possible solutions and improvements. It also summarizes what we know about these birds and conveys something of their wide appeal. It is not an exhaustive, detailed reference work, but rather an introduction to hawks, eagles, falcons, vultures and the rest, aimed at stimulating an interest in them, their study and their welfare. Most of all, this book hopes to promote a deeper understanding of these remarkable creatures.

Above : Verreaux's Eagles at home : the female watches as the male comes in to land, while the single youngster calls

Right : Two Steppe Eagles – scavengers as well as killers of live prey

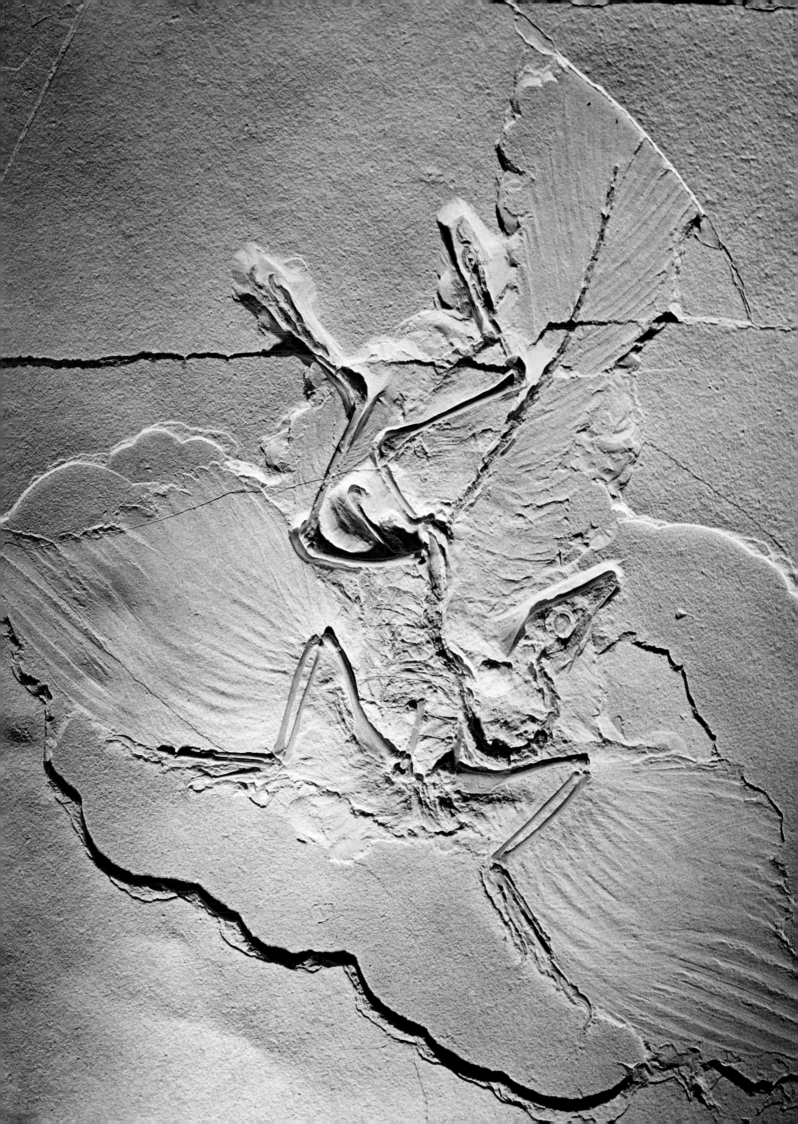

Evolution and the Fossil Record

Left : Fossil remains of Archaeopteryx lithographica, *the earliest known bird. Several reptilian features can be seen—the long tail with its 20 vertebrae, three 'fingers' with claws, ribs and a simple backbone—but note also the clear impression of the wing-feathers which are exactly like those of a modern bird*

More than a century has passed since the theory of evolution caused one of the greatest revisions of thought in the history of biology. Since those first stormy years of argument and debate the principles behind the theory have gained general acceptance and much has been learned. In spite of many yawning gaps in the fossil record, a great deal has been discovered about how earlier creatures lived and how, over millions of years, modern species evolved. The history of birds in general, and birds of prey in particular, is fragmentary, however, and even the main evolutionary trends are little understood. Even so, it is possible to present a summary of what is known so far.

Birds had their origins in the Mesozoic era, having evolved from reptilian ancestors—probably small dinosaurs called Thecodonts. The earliest recognizable bird, the warm-blooded *Archaeopteryx*, lived during the Jurassic period of this era, roughly 160 million years ago. There is then a considerable gap in the fossil record until the Cretaceous period of 70 to 100 million years ago, from which more forms are known, but during the ensuing Eocene period birds seem to have become more numerous and varied: the earliest known bird of prey dates from this time. Birds developed still further during the Pliocene and Pleistocene periods (up to 11 million years ago) and appear to have reached a peak about 500,000 years ago when the number of living species is believed to have been greater by about one third than it is today.

The oldest bird of prey discovered so far is *Lithornis*, found in Eocene London Clay and dated at some 60 million years old. It was a vulturine bird and some authorities consider it to be a member of the Sub-order whose only living representatives are the New World condors and vultures. The oldest American member of this group found so far is *Neocathartes*, also dating from Eocene deposits and apparently a ground-living bird of prey.

Most other types appeared during the Oligocene period, 25 to 40 million years ago, but little is known about which forms came first and their pattern of evolution remains a matter for speculation. As with all groups of birds, the fossil record only tells us part of the story. Perhaps future finds will fill some of the gaps in our knowledge and elucidate some of the many remaining mysteries.

Many interesting fossil finds have been made, and those of the famous Rancho la Brea tar pits near Los Angeles merit special attention. Here, among the traces of numerous Pleistocene animals, many bird remains were found. These show that the near-extinct California Condor, or something very like it, was living in the area perhaps a million years ago. Today a tiny, relict population survives in the mountains not far away. Here, too, an even larger bird of a similar type was found, *Teratornis*, which is believed to have weighed about 50 pounds (22·5 kg) and to have had a wingspan of from 12 to 14 feet (3·6 to 4·2 m). Even more astonishing is yet another similar bird, identified from a single bone, which was larger still.

In considering the existing birds of prey it is important to realize that their family relationships with one another and with their largely unknown predecessors are only partly understood. Their evolution is like a jigsaw puzzle with plenty of pieces which fit together easily

enough but with so many more missing that the final picture remains largely conjectural. Authorities differ, but we can at least attempt some generalized groupings and draw some tentative conclusions.

Since we shall be speaking about Order, Genus, and other groupings, we should at the outset explain the system of classification and nomenclature in universal use. To separate them from other life-forms, all birds are grouped within the Class Aves and this in turn is split into a number of Orders in which related families of birds are placed together. All the penguins are placed in one Order, all the geese, swans and ducks in another, and so on. All birds of prey belong to the Order Falconiformes, which is further broken down into Sub-orders. In their classic work on the world's birds of prey, Brown and Amadon recognized three Sub-orders, and their classification and nomenclature is used throughout this book. These Sub-orders are the Cathartae (New World vultures), the Accipitres (kites, hawks, eagles and Old World vultures) and the Falcones (the falcons and cara-caras). Each Sub-order then consists of families, and each family comprises one or more genera (genus in the singular). A genus brings together

very closely-related birds and consists of one or more species. At species level, each bird has its Latinized 'scientific name' – in theory accepted universally and precluding any confusion over the often ambiguous colloquial names. The way in which these names apply can be seen in the appendix at the end of this book. It will be seen that each name consists of two words – which together form the 'specific name' – and that all the species grouped together within a genus share the same first word.

The Sub-order Cathartae (the New World vultures), derive from the oldest known types of birds of prey. Their ancestors, including *Lithornis*, were also found in Europe, where none are present today. They differ anatomically from other birds of prey and their relationships with them, if any, are most obscure.

Even more problems arise with the evolution of the largest Sub-order, the Accipitres. The diversity of types included in this Sub-order is considerable and only a tentative outline of their evolution and inter-relationships is possible. Since birds of prey probably evolved from scavengers and carrion-feeders, the kites, which generally fall within that category, are usually regarded as the most primitive or 'basic' birds

Above : The colourful King Vulture from the American tropics is a member of the Sub-order Cathartae. These New World vultures seem to be closely related to Lithornis, the oldest known bird of prey

Above right : The 'true' eagles, such as this Tawny Eagle, represent the peak of development in the Sub-order Accipitres

Right : Lanner Falcon from the third Sub-order, the Falcones

within the Sub-order. Two main lines of evolutionary development seem to have stemmed from them, one leading to the Old World vultures and the sea eagles and the other producing, in an approximate evolutionary order of ascendancy, the snake-eagles, the harriers and their allies, the goshawks and their close relatives, the many and diverse buzzards, the harpy eagles and the 'true' eagles. This sub-order also includes the Osprey, a bird which shows some similarities to kites and other hawks, but which has many anatomical peculiarities. The specialized and unique Secretary Bird is also generally classified as a member of the Sub-order Accipitres.

The third Sub-order, the Falcones, divides conveniently into two main groups. The first contains the caracaras and the various falcons of South America which cannot be included in other groups and are known as 'aberrant falcons'. The second includes the small tropical falconets and the true falcons. All these birds seem to be allied to those of the previous Sub-order, but how closely is a matter of opinion. A relationship between falcons and owls has been suggested, but if one exists it is very remote and so this theory is usually discounted.

The Falconiformes

In general terms, the expression 'bird of prey' would fit any species of bird which kills other animals for food, especially perhaps the higher forms of vertebrates. More specifically and in the language of the naturalist it refers to a member of the Order Falconiformes. These go by a variety of names, but the Order takes in hawks, harriers, kites, buzzards, eagles, vultures, falcons and many others. Essentially, they are all either killers of other creatures or at least feed upon the carcasses of other creatures. In addition, they all have hooked bills and, mostly, well-developed feet armed with strong talons for killing. A bird of prey can therefore be a scavenger or a carrion-feeder just as well as it can be a bird-killing hawk or an eagle which feeds on mammals. Even a curiosity like the Palm Nut Vulture qualifies for inclusion, despite its largely vegetarian diet. Currently, the word 'raptor' enjoys wide usage: it is synonymous with 'bird of prey'.

Speaking literally, owls are also birds of prey, but in practice they are usually distinguished as 'nocturnal birds of prey'. While they, too, are armed with hooked bills and have powerful feet with very sharp, large talons, and kill and eat a very wide variety of living creatures, they are anatomically distinct in many ways from the diurnal birds of prey of the Order Falconiformes and may not be very closely related to them at all. They are classified in a separate Order, the Strigiformes, and are not included here.

Birds of prey are found in virtually every major habitat. The only continent where they do not occur is Antarctica, and elsewhere they are only absent from relatively small land areas, such as certain Polynesian islands, and from the open sea. They occur in all but the very coldest regions as well as in the hottest extremes of the tropics, in dense forest and open desert and even on the highest mountain ranges. As we shall see, they are physically adapted to hunt and kill an astonishingly wide variety of prey, from small insects to quite large mammals. Some are capable of catching even the swiftest-flying birds, including in some cases their own relatives, while others are specialists in hunting bats, fish, snakes and a number of other unlikely creatures. To a greater extent than is often realized, many more raptors than simply vultures scavenge or utilize carrion—in some areas even the noble Golden Eagle is as much at home on a dead sheep as a vulture might be elsewhere.

The variation within the Order Falconiformes is considerable and scientists divide it into three Sub-orders: the Cathartae, the Accipitres and the Falcones. Each of these three Sub-orders consists of related species of birds which are grouped into genera and families. This chapter gives a brief outline of the main features of these families and genera, concentrating on geographical distribution and feeding habits. For reference purposes all the species involved are listed in an appendix at the end of the book.

Sub-order Cathartae

The seven New World vultures comprise the Sub-order Cathartae. They are principally carrion-feeders, although the eggs and young of birds, young animals and even fruit may also be eaten occasionally. Some are numbered among the most magnificent fliers of all birds of prey.

The three species of turkey vulture are medium-large birds of mainly open habitats. The common Turkey Vulture ranges from southern Canada to Tierra del Fuego and the Falkland Islands. The stockier, shorter-winged Black Vulture is found from the warmer parts of the United States south to Patagonia, while the colourful King Vulture is chiefly a bird of tropical forest country found from Mexico to northern Argentina.

Of all the cathartids, the two great condors are perhaps the most spectacular. The gigantic Andean Condor, which may weigh more than 25 pounds (11 kg) and have a wingspan of 10 feet (3 m) or even more, is the largest of all birds of prey and certainly ranks among the most famous of all birds. Although it is scarce in some parts of its range, it occurs throughout the length of the Andes, frequently at very high altitudes but also at sea-level in the southern part of the chain. Of almost equal size, the magnificent California Condor has achieved fame as one of the world's rarest birds, now surviving only in its stronghold in the southern coastal mountains of California, where perhaps 50 are still living, and possibly in very small numbers in the remote mountains of Baja California where evidence of the birds' presence has been found in recent years.

Left : An unusual feature of the Turkey Vultures is their ability to locate food partly by smell

Below : American Black Vultures scavenging on the shoreline. Not all birds of prey kill to eat—many, apart from the vultures of the Old and New Worlds, are scavengers and carrion-feeders

Sub-order Accipitres

Above : Adult Osprey and young on a ground nest in Australia. The Osprey is a specialist fisherman with an almost world-wide distribution, occurring on both inland and coastal waters

Right : The Snail or Everglade Kite is a highly specialized member of the kite group, feeding exclusively on water snails. It is found in Florida, Cuba and parts of Central and South America

The Sub-order Accipitres contains three families. The first (Pandionidae) has only one member, the Osprey, which superficially resembles a small eagle, but in fact has many anatomical differences from all other raptors. It is a bird of lakes, rivers and coastal waters, with an almost world-wide distribution, and is the most specialized of all the birds of prey in its ability to catch fish.

The kites belong to the large family Accipitridae, along with the hawks, eagles and Old World vultures. The term 'kite' covers a number of genera containing over 30 species of varied types, all less predatory than most raptors.

The bazas or cuckoo-falcons are smallish kites, crested and long-winged, found chiefly in forest areas in the southern half of Africa, Madagascar, parts of southern and south-eastern Asia and northern Australasia. Their chief food is small reptiles and insects, but some species also take small mammals and birds and even bats. A somewhat similar but larger bird is the Grey-headed or Cayenne Kite of the lowlands of tropical America, which feeds on insects and frogs and, like the Honey Buzzard, has a decided liking for wasp larvae.

Among the specialist kites, the Hook-billed Kite, another tropical American bird, is principally a feeder on land snails, while the Snail Kite itself – which belongs to a separate genus – is even more specialized and eats water snails exclusively, having a specially long, hooked bill with which to pierce and extract the snail as it emerges from its shell. This latter bird is found in parts of Central and South America, Cuba, and Florida (where it is a rarity and known as the Everglade Kite) and is closely related to the Slender-billed Kite of South America. Yet another specialist, of a quite different kind, is the Bat Hawk of Asia and tropical Africa, a falcon-like bird which hunts at dusk and in the early morning over all kinds of open areas, catching small bats and birds such as swifts and swallows with amazing speed and dexterity.

The nests of wasps and bees, with their larvae, honey and adult insects, are the favoured prey of the Honey Buzzard, though other large insects, small mammals and reptiles also feature in its diet. It is a fairly large member of the kite group, superficially resembling a buzzard, and is one of the most variable in plumage of all birds of prey. Another rather similar species, the Barred Honey Buzzard, occurs in the Island of Celebes, Indonesia, and in the Philippines. The Long-tailed and Black Honey Buzzards of New Guinea and New Britain respectively are actually less specialized birds of a different genus.

Perhaps the most striking of all the kites is the beautiful and graceful Swallow-tailed Kite of the Americas. In the United States it is now found commonly only in Florida, but its range to the south extends from Mexico to Argentina. It feeds exclusively on the wing, when its long, forked tail adds considerably to its mobility, catching insects, and also dropping swiftly into trees to snatch up eggs, nestlings, snakes and lizards. The African Swallow-tailed Kite is more closely related to the *Elanus* kites than to the previous species, and is a much smaller but equally delightful bird of semi-desert and savannah. Although mainly an insect feeder, it too will readily take small mammals and reptiles.

The tiny Pearl Kite is rather like a falcon in general appearance and is a bird of open woodland and savannah in South America. As well as insects, it will prey on lizards and small birds – the latter are not usually taken by kites.

Four small, long-winged kites with rather short, rounded tails comprise the genus *Elanus*.

Above : American Swallow-tailed Kites, graceful and agile birds which feed on flying insects and small birds and reptiles taken from the tree-tops

Right : Centuries ago the beautiful Red Kite scavenged the streets of London – but today it is a bird of wooded country

Top left : Black Kites
are 'classic' members of
the kite group–
medium sized (18 to 25
inches or 45–60 cm)
scavengers which will
eat more or less
anything. They occur
from Europe and Africa
eastwards through Asia
to Australia

Far left : The Palm Nut
Vulture or Vulturine
Fish Eagle is a curious
bird, feeding largely on
the husks of oil palm
nuts and apparently
represents an
intermediate stage
between the sea eagles
and the Old World
vultures

Left : Crested Honey
Buzzard taking flight.
Honey Buzzards are
medium-large members
of the kite group (20
to 24 inches or 50–60
cm). Wasps, bees and
their larvae are their
favourite prey

All have somewhat similar grey, black and white plumages and share similar prey and hunting techniques. They are birds of open country, hunting from conspicuous perches or on the wing–when they frequently hover–and eating small mammals, reptiles, small birds and insects. The White-tailed Kite occurs in the southern United States and South America, the Black-shouldered from Africa to southern Asia, with an outpost in Portugal, and the Australian Black-shouldered and the Letter-winged in Australia.

The Double-toothed and Rufous-thighed Kites are both small, short-winged birds of the tropical lowland forests of Central and South America. They are rather sluggish birds, feeding on insects and lizards, and unlike the more graceful, long-winged Plumbeous and Mississippi Kites of the genus *Ictinia*, birds which are chiefly aerial hunters of flying insects. The Plumbeous Kite ranges from Mexico south to Argentina, while the Mississippi Kite is found in the central and southern parts of the United States.

Two closely related kites occur in Australia. The Square-tailed Kite is a harrier-like bird of scrub and open country, while the Black-breasted Buzzard Kite, also a bird of open habitats, is like a buzzard in general appearance and is capable of tackling larger prey up to the size of rabbits.

Perhaps the most representative kites are the two large, long-winged *Milvus* species and the closely related *Haliastur* kites. The well-known Black Kite is a familiar and widespread scavenger, which will eat almost anything. It

The Brahminy Kite of India, south-east Asia and northern Australasia shows a strong liking for the proximity of water where it feeds on fish, crabs, frogs, insects, small snakes and assorted scraps. It is a large kite, as is the closely related Whistling Hawk of Australia which also likes wet areas. This, too, takes a wide variety of prey, up to rabbit size, and is a confirmed carrion-eater.

Eight large birds make up the genus *Haliaeetus*, the sea eagles, which are cosmopolitan except that none occur in South America. All are competent at catching fish, but the little-known Sanford's Sea Eagle of the Solomon Islands is mainly a mammal and bird feeder. Pallas' Sea Eagle, from Central Asia, is essentially an all-round feeder on large inland lakes and rivers, while the handsome and noisy African Fish Eagle occurs both in these habitats and along the coast. The latter is replaced by the very similar Madagascar Fish Eagle on the island of Malagasy, formerly known as Madagascar. In Australasia the genus is represented by the White-bellied Sea Eagle, which has a range extending westwards through south China to India, and which feeds on fish and sea-snakes. The emblem of the United States is the Bald Eagle, a large and impressive bird with a wide range of animal prey and the carrion-feeding and piratical habits of many of the sea eagles. Greenland, northern and south-eastern Europe and much of northern Asia comprise the range of the White-tailed Sea Eagle or Erne, another large and powerful member of the group. The largest and most magnificent of all these birds is Steller's Sea Eagle from the coasts of north-east Asia. It is said to be a very active and powerful bird able to deal with prey up to the size of Arctic Foxes and young seals.

The Grey-headed and Lesser Fishing Eagles are closely allied to the sea eagles, but are specialist fishermen which, like the Osprey, have long, curved talons and rough spicules on the lower surfaces of their toes to enable them to catch and hold their wet, slippery prey. These are freshwater birds, and are found in the area from India across to the Philippines.

The curious Palm Nut Vulture or Vulturine Fish Eagle is thought to provide an evolutionary link to the Old World vultures from the sea eagles. Externally it resembles the sea eagles, but the structure of its bones, and its small, bare head link it to the Egyptian Vulture. Because of these conflicting details it is placed on its own, in the genus *Gypohierax*. It occurs in savannah and forest over those areas of western, central and eastern Africa where the oil

Above: Bald Eagles photographed in Alaska. These are typical of a group of eight large, powerful species known as sea eagles

Overleaf: Old World vultures are medium to very large scavengers and carrion-feeders. Three African species are shown: African White-backed Vulture (left), Rüppell's Griffon (centre) and Lappet-faced Vulture (right)

is found from Europe and Africa eastwards through southern Asia to south China, New Guinea and Australia, and, in the developing countries, is a common bird around human settlements of all sizes. The beautiful Red Kite was apparently the kite which commonly scavenged the streets of London in past centuries, but it is essentially a bird of wooded country today—even though it retains the scavenging habit at one extreme of its range, in the Cape Verde Islands, off the west coast of Africa. It is chiefly a predator on small mammals, birds, insects and reptiles, readily coming to carrion in autumn and winter. It occurs over much of Europe, Asia Minor and north-west Africa, and a relict British population of some 60 birds survives in central Wales.

palm *Elaeis guineensis* is found. The husks of the nuts of this tree are its favourite food, but this largely vegetarian raptor also takes crabs, molluscs, fish and locusts.

Fourteen species of vulture occur in the warmer or more remote regions of the Old World. Half of these belong to the genus *Gyps*, which includes the Indian and African White-backed Vultures, the Cape Vulture and the four Griffons, all large to very large vultures which are exclusively carrion-feeders. The Indian Black Vulture is medium-sized and, like all vultures, spends much of the day soaring in search of carrion. Like the White-headed Vulture of Africa, it is a somewhat solitary bird, not given to assembling at carcasses in large numbers as is the case with the Asian and African Griffons. Of all the group, the huge Lappet-faced Vulture of Africa is the least attractive in appearance, with ugly, folded wattles of skin hanging from the sides of its head. It is able to dominate other species at a corpse and kills at least some prey for itself – including, for example, flamingoes and their young at their breeding colonies. In southern Eurasia, the Black Vulture is the dominant bird at a carcass. This huge bird is the largest of all the Old World vultures and one of the biggest of the world's birds of prey. It is comparatively rare in its outposts in southern Europe – and yet may be seen quite easily on the popular Mediterranean holiday island of Majorca.

Over much of Africa south of the Sahara, the small Hooded Vulture is widespread and often very common, especially round towns and villages where it scavenges and eats refuse of all kinds. The small Egyptian Vulture has a similar role in many parts of its wide range – despite its name it is found in southern Europe, the Middle East, India and most of Africa. When feeding at carcasses, both these slightly built vultures are able to obtain small items left over by their larger, more powerful cousins. In addition, the Egyptian Vulture is known to use stones to break open the eggs of ostriches – thus being the only tool-user among birds of prey.

Finally, there is the unique Lammergeier or Bearded Vulture, a vast, long-winged and long-tailed bird quite different in appearance to all other vultures. It is essentially a mountain species, often encountered at extremely high altitudes, with a scattered distribution in parts of southern Europe, the Middle East and Africa, and more numerous in Afghanistan, Tibet and

Above : Lappet-faced Vulture – one of the largest of the Old World vultures

Above right : Lammergeier or Bearded Vulture, a huge bird with a wingspan of up to 9 feet (2.7 m)

Right : Egyptian Vultures – adult flying and young on the ground – are among the smallest members of the group

north India. Few birds of prey can equal the magnificent flight of this great vulture, and none share its habit of smashing bones to obtain their marrow by dropping them from a height onto rocks.

Snakes and lizards feature as prey for a variety of raptors and, as with birds and fish, there are specialists in this type of quarry—a group of snake or serpent eagles. From southern Europe across the Middle East to India the Short-toed Eagle is a characteristic bird of rather open country; it also occurs widely in Africa, where three somewhat similar medium-sized to small snake eagles are also found, ranging between them from open to quite well-forested country. The niche occupied by these four *Circaetus* eagles is filled by five species of *Spilornis* serpent eagles in the region extending from India to the Celebes and Philippines. The Congo Serpent Eagle is a medium-sized, short-winged hawk well adapted to life in the forests of west and central Equatorial Africa. The Madagascar Serpent Eagle, a rare and almost unknown bird, is also a forest hawk.

While undoubtedly a snake hawk, and related to all the birds just mentioned, the extraordinary Bateleur is not like any of them in appearance.

Birds of prey are not usually brightly-coloured, and this bird is one of the few exceptions. It is also virtually tailless in appearance, which, combined with its very long wings, gives it a unique shape as it soars rapidly to and fro across the bush, savannahs and plains of Africa. While it is adept at tackling many reptiles and even tortoises, it also takes small mammals and some birds and, unlike other snake eagles, is partial to carrion.

The African Harrier Hawk is a rather large, long-winged bird of forest habitats, uniquely adept among birds of prey in its agility at climbing around trees and even hanging upside-down when robbing nests of eggs or fledglings. Various insects and small reptiles and mammals are also eaten, as well as the fruits of the oil palm. Another closely-related species is found in Malagasy. In some ways, the habits of these two birds resemble those of the Crane Hawk of Central and South America, a rather short-winged species that feeds on a similar range of prey which it seeks out in holes in rocks and trees and in other vegetation.

Harriers are a cosmopolitan group of medium-sized hawks of open country; all are long in the wing and tail and spend much time flying, patrolling back and forth in search of a variety of small mammals, birds, insects, reptiles and amphibians. There are ten species: the Spotted Harrier occurs in Australia, as does the Marsh Harrier which has a wide distribution, also occurring in Eurasia and North Africa. In the southern half of Africa the latter is replaced by the similar African Marsh Harrier, while the Black Harrier is confined to Natal and Cape Province in South Africa. The Hen Harrier or Marsh Hawk is found widely in Europe and Asia and is the only representative of the genus (*Circus*) in North America, but South America boasts the Long-winged and Cinereous Harriers, the latter also occurring in the Falklands. Montagu's and Pallid are both Eurasian, though the latter does not breed in Western Europe, while Montagu's Harrier also nests in North Africa. Lastly, the handsome Pied Harrier is found in northern Asia and Burma.

Three medium to small African hawks comprise the genus *Melierax*. Two of these, the Dark and Pale Chanting Goshawks, are very alike, though the former is found in woodland and bush habitats, while the latter is more characteristic of semi-desert areas. Both take reptiles and insects on the ground, as well as some mammals

and birds. The Gabar Goshawk is smaller and is a more dashing hunter, resembling a sparrow-hawk both in appearance and in its methods of chasing small birds.

Before considering the large genus *Accipiter*, mention must be made of three species, all from separate genera, which are closely related to the typical bird-hawks. Doria's Goshawk, from New Guinea, is a large forest-hawk, apparently prey-ing mainly on birds, about which very little is known. Much the same can be said of the Red Goshawk of northern Australia, partly because it too is very rare and is seldom observed. It is a longer-winged bird, suited to life in open woodland and scrub where it feeds chiefly on medium-sized birds. The African Long-tailed Hawk is found in the forests of west Africa, and preys chiefly on squirrels and small birds caught in the treetops. Apart from its excep-tionally long tail, this bird closely resembles those of the standard *Accipiter* type.

The world-wide genus *Accipiter* contains 47 species. These are the sparrowhawks and gos-hawks, to give them their most common group names. Sparrowhawks are mostly rather small, long-legged birds while goshawks are larger and more powerful. All species have relatively short wings and longish tails which serve them per-fectly for hunting in thick cover where they can operate with astonishing speed and agility. For the most part, these species are bird-hawks, con-centrating more on avian prey than most other raptorial birds, but some species also take mam-mals, especially tree-living squirrels, while others feed on assorted reptiles and amphibians, insects and even snails. Unfortunately, a few are also proficient poultry-killers. Many birds of prey show a marked disparity in size between the sexes, the female being the larger, and this trait is more marked in the genus *Accipiter* than in any other. Indeed, in some species some females may actually weigh twice as much as their mates.

The Northern Goshawk is basically represen-tative of the larger types – a buzzard-sized forest-hawk, fully capable of taking prey up to grouse size and an efficient hunter of mammals such as rabbits and squirrels, it is found across much of northern Eurasia and in North America. In many ways the African and Australian Goshawks are its equivalent species in those two regions. Another Australian species, the White or Grey Goshawk, is of special interest in that some in-dividuals are pure white throughout their lives.

Above: Sharp-shinned Hawk, a typical small sparrowhawk of the genus Accipiter *– a dashing bird-hunter, short-winged and long-tailed, adapted to hunting in woodland and thick cover*

Right: The Northern Goshawk is a powerful, fast-moving hunter found in woodlands and forests across much of Eurasia and North America. The adult female is a large bird, as can be seen from the size of the dead pigeon in this illustration

Left : The Grasshopper Buzzard Eagle (14 to 16 inches or 35–40 cm) is a long-winged hawk of open country. It is largely insectivorous but also takes some lizards and small mammals

favours insects as its prey, though no doubt it takes some lizards and small mammals as do the White-eyed Buzzard and the other two Asian species, the Grey-faced and the Rufous-winged Buzzard Eagles. The Grey-faced Buzzard Eagle inhabits more wooded terrain than the others, all of which are essentially birds of open country.

The small Lizard Buzzard of Africa is a bird of well-wooded areas too, with a preference for lizards, caught on the ground or from trees, rocks and walls–though it will readily take snakes, small mammals, large insects and birds.

A group of medium to rather small buzzard-like hawks are found in tropical Central and South America: these are the ten species of the genus *Leucopternis*. All are birds of forests or at least well-timbered areas and feed mainly on lizards and snakes, but in fact very little is known of their habits. Like many South American raptors they would be worthy of further study. The best known seems to be the conspicuous and handsome White Hawk, a fairly common bird found from southern Mexico to Brazil.

The Common Black Hawk of the genus *Buteo-gallus* occurs from the south-west of the United States to the northern parts of South America as well as in the West Indian Islands of the Antilles and on Cuba. In most areas it is a bird of coastal lowlands and feeds on reptiles, crabs, frogs, fish, insects and small mammals. The rather similar Great Black Hawk of the American tropics takes much the same sort of prey and is also fond of water, while the Rufous Crab Hawk from the lowland swamps of the coastal parts of Venezuela is the most specialized of the three and feeds entirely on crabs.

From Mexico well into South America, the large Black Solitary Eagle occurs on hill slopes and mountains, including those with forest cover. Again, little is known about this splendid bird, although it certainly feeds on snakes and some medium-sized birds. The Crowned Solitary Eagle of the same genus, *Harpyhaliaetus*, is also South American, occurring in open and thinly wooded country where it apparently feeds mainly on small mammals, birds and probably snakes.

The grasslands with scattered pools and marshes found over a wide area from Panama south to Argentina are favoured by the Savannah Hawk, a long-winged, long-legged bird which hunts a wide variety of prey, including reptiles, fish, and small mammals. On the other hand the attractively coloured, thick-set Fishing Buzzard is a specialist feeder in wetland habitats, taking fish from the water and not infrequently plunging in after them. It is a fairly common

This phenomenon is known as a white colour phase. It is unique among accipiters–though some species have dark phases.

Equally, the small European Sparrowhawk, or the similar Cooper's and Sharp-shinned Hawks of North America, are typical of the many sparrowhawks found around the world – dashing, bold little hunters, feeding on birds taken on the wing or from the ground, plus a small proportion of small mammals and lizards. Many species take lizards on the ground, and the Spot-tailed Accipiter of the Celebes Island of Indonesia seems to be a specialist in this respect. In the mountains of the same island the rare Celebes Little Sparrowhawk is known to take snails. The African Little Sparrowhawk is a most proficient catcher of flying insects, as are some other members of the genus. Perhaps the most specialized of all is the Grey Frog Hawk of Korea and eastern China–many accipiters will occasionally hunt in the open, but this species does so almost exclusively in search of its particular prey.

Moving on to the genus *Butastur*, we find four species of medium-sized, long-winged hawks from Africa and tropical Asia. As its name suggests, the Grasshopper Buzzard Eagle

bird of tropical lowland areas from Mexico to Argentina and Paraguay.

A large, broad-winged bird of the uplands of western South America and lower-lying country south to Tierra del Fuego, the Grey Eagle-buzzard is a mammal feeder, also taking some insects and carrion. It is probably closely allied to the hawks of the genus *Buteo*, as is the Bay-winged Hawk, a medium-sized, long-winged bird of open or partially open country found from the south-western United States into South America. While it feeds mainly on rodents, this bird is also an agile bird-catcher and probably catches a good many lizards.

The genus *Buteo*–known as buzzards in Europe, hawks or buteos in America–is made up of 25 broad-winged, mainly medium-sized hawks, all highly efficient at soaring, and feeding on a very wide range of prey. This group is believed to have evolved in South America and indeed the New World boasts all but eight of the 25 species. The smallish Grey Hawk, found from Arizona to South America, and the Roadside Hawk (Mexico to Argentina) are the most primitive buzzards, related perhaps to the *Leucopternis* group mentioned above, while five medium to small species, including the Red-shouldered, Broad-winged and Short-tailed Hawks of some parts of the United States form a

Left : Harpy Eagle, one of several very large (36 to 40 inches or 91–100 cm), short-winged forest eagles. It occurs in Central and South America and feeds mainly on tree-living mammals, including monkeys and opossums

Above: The Booted Eagle of Eurasia and North Africa is a hawk-eagle of lightly-wooded and often hilly country. A dashing hunter, it preys on small to medium-sized mammals and birds

sub-group of birds favouring well-timbered habitats. Another sub-group consists of five larger, open country hawks of the New World, and includes Swainson's Hawk of North America and the versatile Galapagos Hawk.

Among the remaining members of the genus are the handsome Zone-tailed Hawk of the south-western United States and parts of Central America, the Red-tailed and Ferruginous Hawks, also North American, and all the Old World species. The well-known Common Buzzard is widespread in its many forms across Eurasia, while the Rough-legged Buzzard, from Arctic and sub-Arctic regions, is unique in that it breeds in both the Old World and the New. Migrants apart, Africa has three species, with a fourth in Malagasy. The Hawaiian Buzzard is found only on Hawaii where it now feeds widely on the rats introduced by human beings, after having presumably been insectivorous in earlier times.

The true eagles form a large and varied group, of which the first four species of very large, rather short-winged forest eagles are particularly splendid representatives even if relatively little known in the wild. The huge and immensely powerful Harpy Eagle of Central and South America feeds mainly on tree-living mammals, including monkeys and opossums. Slightly smaller but equally striking in appearance is the Guiana Crested Eagle, no doubt the Harpy Eagle's close relative and similarly skilled in the capture of arboreal prey. Both may well be related to two relict species, the New Guinea Harpy Eagle–probably the least known of the four–and the huge Philippine Monkey-eating Eagle which is now one of the rarest and most endangered birds of prey in the world.

The exact evolutionary position of the unusual Indian Black Eagle is a matter of debate–but this long-winged bird is at least a true eagle in appearance. From India to the East Indies it frequents wooded terrain in mountains, where it hunts at a peculiarly slow, leisurely pace in search of birds' eggs and their young–although it also takes some of the smaller mammals and birds.

Curiously, to many bird-watchers the genus *Aquila* alone signifies real eagles, which is hardly fair to the many fine eagles of other genera. But the nine or ten species are impressive-looking, medium to large in size with long, broad wings, and some of them are among the most superb fliers of all birds of prey. The group

35

includes some spectacular hunters, preying on a variety of mammals and birds, as well as some which will feed on carrion and at least one which is often a true scavenger.

The most famous is the Golden Eagle, a mountain species of Eurasia and North America and one of the most closely-studied of all birds of prey. In Africa its place is taken by the most handsome member of the genus, Verreaux's Eagle. The largest is the Imperial Eagle, also Eurasian, a bird of open plains whose Spanish race is numbered among Europe's scarcest birds of prey. Eurasia is also the home of the two Spotted Eagles, rather small species of well-timbered habitats, while in Africa Wahlberg's Eagle is the *Aquila* of savannah and bushveld. Tawny and Steppe Eagles—which are treated as separate species by some but as one by others—are essentially birds of open country at lower altitudes and are more prone to carrion-feeding and general scavenging than the others. Occurring in New Guinea and on some other islands in that region, Gurney's Eagle is certainly the least known of the group, while the big Wedge-tailed Eagle of Australia is perhaps the most notorious through its largely unjustified reputation as a killer of lambs.

A number of small or medium-sized eagles are called, collectively, hawk-eagles, although they are placed in four different genera. There are five *Hieraaetus* eagles—dashing, long-winged birds of lightly-wooded areas. Bonelli's Eagle is Eurasian, with a separate race in Africa called the African Hawk-eagle. In North Africa and Eurasia there is the Booted Eagle and, in Australia and New Guinea, the Little Eagle. All are killers of small to medium-sized mammals and birds. On the other hand, the handsome Chestnut-bellied Hawk-eagle of India and south-east Asia feeds mainly on fairly large forest birds, while in Africa Ayres' Hawk-eagle preys on smaller birds.

In the tropics of the New World, the attractive Black and White Hawk-eagle occurs, but is little known, although it is no doubt capable of preying on medium-sized mammals and birds. Small mammals are the main diet of the curious-looking Long-crested Eagle of Africa, but small reptiles and large insects are also taken.

The ten members of the genus *Spizaetus* vary in size from small to quite large. All are basically forest birds, with rather short wings, and many are crested. Their prey includes a range of small to medium-sized mammals and birds, varying

Above left : Often a rather tame bird, and very characteristic of African roadsides, the Long-crested Eagle feeds on small mammals, reptiles and insects

Above : The impressive Martial Eagle (32 to 38 inches or 81–96 cm), is the largest of all the African eagles, and can tackle small antelopes

Right : Threat display from a falconer's Crowned Eagle. This large and very powerful eagle is typical of a number of big, short-winged forest eagles which prey on medium-sized birds and mammals such as monkeys

according to the size of the eagle, but, in the case of the various species found in the region from south-east Asia to Borneo, little is known of their life and habits. Much the same is true of the only African species, Cassin's Hawk-eagle. The Mountain Hawk-eagle of Asia is the largest and most powerful of the group while one of the two tropical New World species, the Ornate Hawk-eagle, is often regarded as one of the most handsomely coloured of all raptors.

Three big, impressive eagles remain to be mentioned. Isidor's Eagle is a large, robust bird of the forested slopes of the Andes, probably eating arboreal mammals and birds for the most part. The Martial Eagle is the largest African eagle, fully capable of tackling prey as big as bustards, guinea fowl and small antelopes and,

sometimes, poultry. The slightly smaller Crowned Eagle, also African but a shorter-winged forest species, is similarly a very powerful bird and feeds almost entirely on mammals, including some monkeys and small antelopes.

Although its systematic position is debatable (it is possibly related to the cranes), the unique Secretary Bird is normally treated as a bird of prey, and placed in a separate family, the Sagittariidae. It is large and eagle-like, but is also long-legged and almost wholly a ground-living predator. In the open country which it always frequents, it preys on small mammals and insects for the most part, plus a few birds and reptiles. While it has a fully justified reputation as a competent snake-killer, these are not normally a major item of prey.

Above : The long-legged, ground-dwelling Secretary Bird has long puzzled zoologists : while it is generally classified as a bird of prey, some authorities believe it is related to the cranes

Sub-order Falcones

Moving on to the Sub-order Falcones, we find four main groups: the caracaras, the forest falcons, the falconets and the so-called true falcons of the genus *Falco*.

Caracaras are New World birds, mostly from Central and South America, which are generally found in open to lightly-timbered habitats. They vary in size from small and slight to quite large and robust, but most have relatively weak bills and claws and are well adapted to spending quite a lot of time on the ground. As a group, they take a wide range of small prey and several are partly vegetarian. Equally, many are notable scavengers and carrion-feeders, and some have a reputation for attacking weak and sickly livestock, even up to the size of a full-grown sheep. The Common Caracara is a large, vigorous and piratical bird which will eat virtually anything. This species occurs in the southern United States and is also the national bird of Mexico. One of the tropical, arboreal species, the Red-throated Caracara, is a specialist in its food preferences, favouring wasp larvae and raiding wasps' nests with impunity.

Another specialist and the first of the aberrant falcons is the short-winged, large-headed and rather sluggish Laughing Falcon, an interesting bird found in wooded areas of the tropical New World. It feeds on snakes, even including large or venomous ones, and lizards. This bird is perhaps related to the forest falcons of the genus *Micrastur*, also from tropical parts of Central and South America. These vary in size, but all are short-winged woodland hunters, probably preying on birds chiefly, although it is known that the Collared Forest Falcon also takes small mammals and reptiles. Provisionally, five species are recognized, of which two are rare and one is virtually unknown.

Falconets are very small birds of prey with a tropical distribution. Their only New World representative is the Spot-winged Falconet, a bird of savannah and semi-desert in Argentina, again a little known species but one which is said to feed on small birds. In Africa, there is the African Pigmy Falcon, a bird of dry, rather open country, largely insectivorous but also taking some small birds and mammals. Fielden's Falconet of south-west Asia is rather similar. The five tiny *Microhierax* species are found in the region from India to the Philippines; all are quite boldly coloured and occur in wooded habitats of varying densities where their chief prey is insects. Some also take small mammals and birds, especially the largest of the genus, the Pied Falconet, which is also known to eat small reptiles.

Finally, there is the large genus *Falco*—the true falcons. This contains 37 species, with long, pointed wings, strong, toothed bills and generally short legs.

All the kestrels are basically similar: small falcons of mainly open country, many with the very distinctive habit of hovering while hunting. Although several species take tiny birds and reptiles regularly, small mammals and insects of various sizes comprise their chief prey. Included in the group are many island species, doubtless all closely related, one of which, the Mauritius Kestrel, has the distinction of being virtually the world's rarest bird. It seems to be on the verge of extinction and certainly less than ten birds were alive in 1974. The Common Kestrel

of Eurasia and Africa is one of the best known species (and is by far the most familiar bird of prey in Britain), and throughout the New World the American Kestrel—often confusingly called 'Sparrowhawk'—has much the same status. The gregarious Red-footed Falcon of Eurasia is closely related to the kestrels.

Merlins, or Pigeon-hawks as they are often called in the United States, are widespread in open, barren habitats in northern Europe, Asia and North America and are small, fast-flying bird-catchers. In India and Africa a similar bird, the Red-headed Merlin fills a comparable niche and also takes ground-living prey such as lizards.

The hobby group includes about a dozen species of very agile, fast-flying falcons, found from Europe and Africa across Asia to Australia, which capture most of their prey on the wing. Many of them are insectivorous—and like other birds of prey with a similar diet often hunt at dusk—and many are capable of outflying and capturing the fastest-flying and most agile of small birds, such as swallows and swifts. In Europe and Asia, the European Hobby is perhaps the best known species. Eleonora's Falcon of the Mediterranean region is also worth mentioning—this is a gregarious species which nests late and is able to feed its young on small migrant birds which pass through the region in great numbers in autumn. Some species such as the curious, long-legged Brown Hawk of Australia and the handsome Aplomado Falcon of the Americas, take mammal and reptile prey from the ground, while another New World species,

Top left : The curious Laughing Falcon feeds mainly on snakes

Above left : The Red-headed Merlin occurs in open country in India and parts of southern Africa

Above : Kestrels are small falcons found in open country, many of which have the distinctive habit of hovering while hunting. The Nankeen Kestrel of Australia and New Guinea is a typical member of the group

Top right : Only 7.5 inches (19 cm) in length, the African Pigmy Falcon is one of the smallest of all birds of prey

Above right : The American Kestrel – also confusingly called a Sparrowhawk – is another typical Kestrel and is one of the most common raptors of the New World

the Bat Falcon, may take bats – a rare prey type for most of the hobby group.

Five medium-sized to very large falcons form the next group. The Lanner Falcon of Africa, south-east Europe and Asia Minor is largely a bird feeder, but the Laggar Falcon of Asia and the Prairie Falcon of the United States take mammals and some reptiles too. Mammals are the main prey of the Eurasian Saker Falcon and also feature – along with birds – among the prey of the Gyrfalcon, the largest and most powerful of the falcons. This last bird, like some other raptors, has a number of colour phases, with birds of different phases occurring in different regions. An almost pure white form is found in Greenland. An Arctic species, this splendid raptor has an almost circumpolar distribution.

Last come the Peregrine and its three close cousins: the Orange-breasted Falcon occurs from Mexico to South America; the Taita Falcon is a rarity from eastern and central Africa; and Kleinschmidt's Falcon is probably one of the least known of all birds of prey – described only from a few specimens at the extreme tip of South America. Without doubt, the Peregrine itself represents a climax in falcon evolution. It is an almost cosmopolitan bird, with many well-defined geographical races, and with its magnificent powers of flight and robust build is surely one of the most efficient hunters in nature. Birds taken in flight, ranging from quite small ones in the case of the Taita Falcon to ducks, crows, grouse and the like in the case of the Peregrine, are the main prey of this group.

Physical Characteristics

The variations among birds of prey are considerable and yet they all conform to a fairly basic pattern and have certain features in common whatever their size, shape, or mode of feeding. Broadly speaking, the majority of them are medium-sized (they could be compared to a domestic chicken) to rather large (about the size of a turkey), but there are extremes at either end of the scale. A male Andean Condor may weigh 25 pounds (11 kg) when fully adult – 250 times as much as the tiny falconets, the smallest members of the Order. Even within families the range can be considerable: among the *Accipitridae*, some of the small sparrowhawks weigh only a few ounces while the biggest species – the Harpy Eagle – might tip the scales at something close to 20 pounds (9 kg).

Anyone who has watched Sparrowhawks or Peregrines, for example, will have noticed a marked difference in size between the sexes. As with owls, females are larger than males in most birds of prey, but the relative difference varies considerably from species to species. It is most marked among the more rapacious and vigorous hunters in the Order, being especially noticeable in the sparrowhawk and goshawk group, some of the larger eagles and the larger falcons and less obvious among the more sluggish hunters and the general scavengers. In species which feed exclusively on carrion, the vultures of the Old and New Worlds, it is often hard to distinguish any size difference at all and with some, including the Andean Condor, the male is actually the larger.

There have been several rather unsatisfactory attempts to explain this. One theory suggests that a size difference enables a pair of birds to make the most efficient use of the range of prey available to them, so that they do not compete with each other for food resources. Another popular explanation concerns nesting habits. It is suggested that the smaller male, who does most of the hunting for the family while the young are newly hatched, brings in suitably small prey while the female takes care of larger items when the young have grown and she can spend time away from the nest. While there may well be some truth in both theories, there is little evidence to show that males habitually take smaller prey than females, or vice versa, and the reason for this size disparity seems to be a more subtle and complex one.

Aggressive and predatory birds which are by nature mainly solitary may even view others of the same species as potential victims, with obvious drawbacks when it comes to pairing and mating. To counterbalance this, nature has evolved courtship displays and ritualized behaviour between male and female aimed at creating and maintaining a pair bond in which appeasement is an important factor. In courtship and mating the male bird of prey assumes the dominant or more aggressive role and it is now believed that the larger size of the female compensates for this so that the aggressive male is suitably cowed and equilibrium is achieved. Thus, the size difference is an adaptation with a survival value in that it facilitates pair formation and the harmonious rearing of a family.

Very few raptors can be described as colourful, and they are among the least brightly-plumaged birds. Nevertheless, many are quite strikingly marked and handsome in their way – consider, for example, the Bateleur, Verreaux's

Eagle, the American Kestrel and the Letter-winged Kite, to name just a few. Many more show beautifully subtle blends of colours in the pattern of their plumage. In this context however, beauty has as much, if not more, to do with shape, movement and flight as with colour.

In most species the sexes are more or less alike in appearance but in some, such as the Hen Harrier and some of the kestrels, there is a conspicuous difference. Camouflage is not a well-developed feature of the Order, although the patterns of some ground-nesting birds are a help in this respect, and the 'counter-shading' principle tends to apply among the more active hunters. This means that the underparts are lighter in colour than the upperparts, rendering the bird of prey less conspicuous to its prey. Many species are crested, while others have very obvious markings, all of which may assume roles in display postures.

Plumage variation within a single species is a common feature in a number of birds of prey, and as a group they show this trend more markedly than most other Orders of birds. These variations are of two kinds, 'individual' and 'geographical', and they may form a distinct pattern against the bird's distribution.

Geographical variation, which is genetically controlled, produces plumage differences in a species in different parts of its range. If we consider part of the Gyrfalcon population as an example, we will find the form commonly called the Greenland Falcon is almost pure white, while the Iceland form is intermediate between this and the greyer, well-marked variety occurring in Arctic Norway.

It is now believed that individual variation may occur as a by-product of genes which control other factors and that any variation of this kind will probably persist if it is not disadvantageous to the species concerned. Individual variation is well known in several species, and may occur as a series of distinct colour phases, where individual birds have distinctive colours throughout their lives. For example, dark and light phases occur in Common and Rough-legged Buzzards, with many intermediate stages, and these may well occur together. In fact, while this book was being written the author saw four Rough-legged Buzzards together, none of which were quite the same in appearance. Rufous, or reddish, phases occur too, as in Ferruginous and Red-tailed Hawks, while a white phase occurs in the Grey Goshawk of Australia. A good example of how individual and geographical variations may form a pattern together is seen in the Red-tailed Hawk of North America whose dark form is rare in the east but common in the west.

Below left : Two Galapagos Hawks, an immature on the left and an adult, show the differences in plumage often found in birds of different ages

As nestlings, birds of prey begin life covered in a thick down which forms their protection against the elements for a relatively long time. There are two types of down, the pre-pennae which precede the normal feathers, and the pre-plumulae which precede the plumules, the tiny, downy feathers which lie beneath the main contour feathering. The times at which these two forms of down appear and the rates at which they are replaced by true feathers vary considerably from species to species. Some small hawks may be growing their first feathers when they are only two or three weeks of age, but the process is slower in bigger birds and in particularly slow developers, like the condors, does not occur until the young bird is two or three months old.

The juvenile plumage which follows is often characterized by pale-tipped or pale-margined feathers and is usually distinct from that of adults, being more obscurely or densely marked in most cases. At this age, those species which show sexual differences as adults look alike—although the American Kestrel is a notable exception to this rule. Small hawks may have moulted into adult dress by the time they are about 15 months old, but 4 or 5 years may pass before large eagles attain a mature appearance and even longer in the case of the big condors.

Moult not only occurs as young birds gradually approach adult plumage but is also a regular process whereby old and worn feathers are replaced. Again, there is considerable variation within the Order. Small hawks usually complete a full moult within six months, but the whole process is much slower and will take two or three years in a large bird like the Golden Eagle. Timing varies too—migrant species, for example, do not moult until after their migration is completed.

Some birds become flightless when moulting —for example many of the ducks and geese—but as one might expect this never happens among raptors, to whom flight is all-important. The primaries, the main flight-feathers, moult in a regular sequence, varying from one group to another but always occurring so that gaps in a wing are minimized and flight is not impaired. For instance, large, soaring birds like eagles and vultures will begin wing-moult in several places at once, but adjacent feathers are never shed at the same time and a new, soft primary is protected as it develops by strong neighbours on either side.

Powerful wings are of the utmost importance to birds of prey, a group to whom maximum mobility when searching for prey is essential. The range of prey eaten is so wide and the sort of terrain where it might be obtained so varied that it comes as no surprise that the raptors use virtually every kind of flight pattern and include some of the most splendid fliers of all birds.

The performance of an airborne bird of prey will vary according to windspeed or turbulence, although many are seen at their best in the most violent air conditions in which, unlike many birds, they are perfectly at home. Streamlining is clearly important to some species. The close-feathered, narrow-winged falcons represent the epitome of design for high-speed flying, in contrast to the bigger, broader-winged eagles and vultures which are built for sustained operations at slower airspeeds. It is worth mentioning, however, that even these big raptors, while not in the same class as the larger falcons, can themselves achieve quite remarkable feats of speed and manoeuvrability.

The most common bird of prey shape is one where the wings are rather short and rounded and the tail quite long. This flight silhouette is as typical of a small sparrowhawk or cuckoo-falcon as it is of the very big and powerful Harpy and Crowned Eagles. Whatever their size, all these birds live and fly in wooded country and not in the open where the longer-winged types occur.

The main types of flight with which we are concerned are flapping, hovering, gliding and soaring, and we shall see how different birds use some or all of these techniques and how their wings and tails are shaped accordingly.

Sustained flapping flight requires longish, rather narrow wings or short, rounded ones if it is not to waste energy. Both types are found in combination with a long tail in the harriers, the sparrowhawks and goshawks. Harriers are highly active, buoyant fliers which hunt over open country, while the short-winged sparrowhawks and goshawks hunt mainly in cover, often at high speed. Both groups intersperse periods of flapping with glides. Their long tails are flexible and aid their powers of manoeuvre, allowing them to change direction, pull up short or mount an attack with split-second timing. Many other species progress with flaps and a series of rather long glides when travelling or hunting. Essentially, flapping consumes a lot of energy, so the more efficiently it can be performed the better. Big, broad-winged birds of prey are much less efficient and place more

reliance on gliding and soaring. When air conditions are unsuitable for them they may prefer not to fly at all, or if they are obliged to do so they often convey an impression of ponderous clumsiness.

Hovering is really an extension of flapping flight, the object of which is to remain stationary in mid-air while prey is searched for below. It is achieved by a gentle beating of the wings through a rather shallow arc, with the body tilted upwards and the tail spread out to give extra lift. The kestrels are the best-known exponents of this specialized kind of flying, but some small kites hover just as readily and expertly. Even among much larger birds, like the Short-toed Eagle and the Rough-legged Buzzard, hovering is an essential part of hunting technique and most other species can hover briefly if the occasion demands.

The most usual mode of progress is gliding, either in travelling, hunting or migrating. All birds of prey glide to some extent, either in between bursts of flapping flight or in a much more prolonged manner. Perhaps the greatest exponent is the huge Lammergeier or Bearded Vulture, a bird of high mountain country which, once under way, glides on and on around mountain contours and rock faces, maintaining or even increasing altitude as it uses the winds and

upcurrents of air. How gliding can be used may be illustrated by imagining one bird on a journey: a Golden Eagle leaves its nest-site on a hunting foray; probably the nest is in a valley, well below the highest point on a cliff, so initially the eagle will use either the updraughts of air in front of this cliff, or perhaps a 'thermal', a vertical current of rising, warmer air, to circle upward until it gains some height and can start travelling. Once aloft, the circling eagle trims its wings from the full-spread, soaring position into gliding order – the tips folded back and the carpal joint angled forwards – closes its tail and sets off across a ridge of hills towards the next valley. Its forward motion in this long glide is now slightly downwards and is provided simply by gravity. Apart from a few deep, heavy flaps when leaving the eyrie, the bird has used no energy so far, and will probably now be travelling at high speed. Eagles travelling in this way may reach 60 miles per hour (96 km/h). On gaining another hill ridge, the bird encounters a new upsurge of air and actually gains height in its long glide. Oddly, a net gain in altitude caused by a combination of the bird's forward speed and the lift it gains in an updraught is not an uncommon phenomenon, even if progress is still made through gravity alone.

Finally, the eagle arrives over the next valley

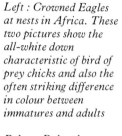

Left : Crowned Eagles at nests in Africa. These two pictures show the all-white down characteristic of bird of prey chicks and also the often striking difference in colour between immatures and adults

Below : Pale colour phases are seen in a number of birds of prey but the most striking example of all is provided by the pure white phase of the Grey Goshawk of Australia

Left : This diagram shows
(a) Warm air rises to form a 'bubble' or 'thermal' in which birds of prey obtain lift and soar effortlessly
(b) Winds meeting a hillside form strong upcurrents of air which many birds of prey use for soaring

Right : Kestrel, showing the main flight feathers

and by closing its wings further reduces lift and glides down at a steeper angle than before to reach the lower slopes and begin hunting. In the space of a few minutes it has travelled perhaps three miles (about 5 km) and used hardly any energy at all.

Events like this are commonplace, and similar if less spectacular journeys can be seen wherever birds of prey occur. In the case of an eagle, or any large bird of prey which may have to cover large areas in search of elusive or often thinly distributed prey, it is clearly advantageous for the bird to be able to travel without loss of energy. Soaring, like gliding, might also provide the solution.

Soaring, too, depends on gravity to achieve forward motion, but lift is the important factor

now as a soaring bird seeks to maintain altitude or, more often, to increase it. Without an ascending air current to provide lift, soaring is impossible. Air forced upwards over a natural feature like a mountain or a hill ridge provides the right conditions, but in flat country and especially in warmer climates, thermals are sought out and used by soaring raptors. It is interesting to note that thermals may take some time to form, so that many birds which rely on thermals for lift will not get aloft until well into the morning when the air has warmed.

While many buzzards, eagles and other birds soar for long periods, and are well equipped to do so with their long, broad wings and short but ample tails, the big vultures and condors are the acknowledged masters in this field. These

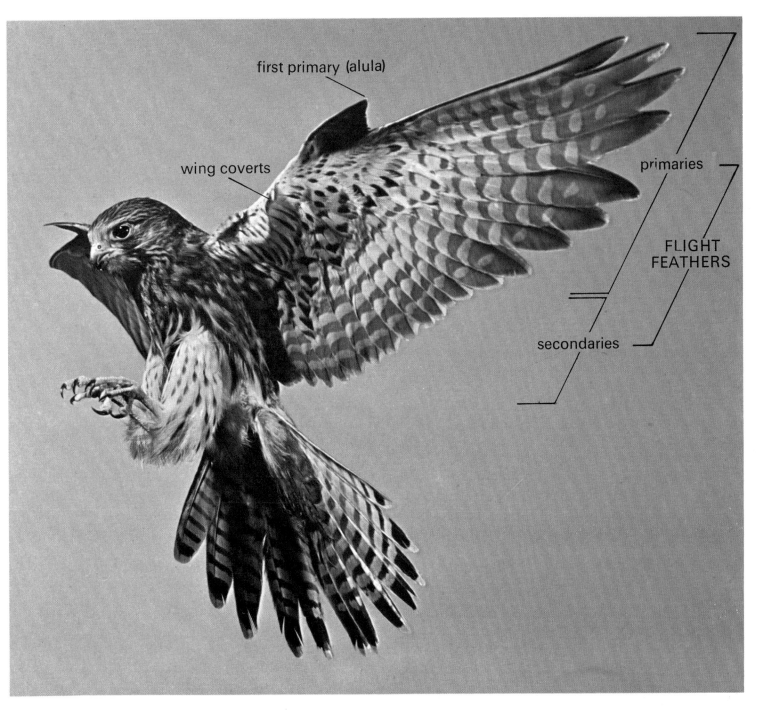

first primary (alula)

wing coverts

primaries

FLIGHT
FEATHERS

secondaries

great birds spend hours on the wing, soaring in slow, wide circles or gliding from one thermal or up-draught to the next in their ceaseless search for carrion. Their wings are very long (up to 10 feet (3m) in span in Andean Condors, and 9 feet (2.7m) in the largest Old World species, the Black Vulture) with long, 'fingered' primaries and elongated secondaries, providing as broad a wing area as possible to gain the lift needed for soaring. Their tails are quite short and when fully fanned their outermost feathers meet the innermost secondaries so that there is a continuous trailing edge from one wing across to the other.

The 'fingered' primaries, so obvious in the vultures and a characteristic feature of virtually all the soaring raptors, are the result of the emargination of these main flight-feathers. The leading edge of each feather is, as it were, cut away and these gaps then form what are in effect wing-slots, presumably to reduce drag and certainly improving the overall efficiency of the wing for soaring. In a very few soaring birds, most notably the Indian Black Eagle, the primaries are long, very soft and only slightly emarginated. This is thought to be an adaptation to facilitate exceptionally slow, circling flight, which is of great benefit to a bird like the Black Eagle which seeks out very small prey in the tops of trees.

Tails are important aids to manoeuvrability, hovering and soaring, and when considering the aerodynamics of birds of prey the function of the tail cannot be ignored. A few raptors have rather special tails: the long and deeply-forked tail of the Red Kite and of the beautiful American Swallow-tailed Kite are highly flexible and allow these birds to manoeuvre slowly and subtly, as they search with great thoroughness for small animals on the ground or in the tree-tops.

The feet and bills of birds of prey form the basis of their killing and feeding apparatus. Contrary to popular belief, those raptors which take live prey almost always capture it and kill it with their feet–or, more accurately, with their toes and the hooked claws or talons with which these are equipped. The nature of the feet and talons varies considerably in relation to the type of prey taken. The thickest, strongest legs and toes and the most vicious-looking talons belong to those birds which capture the largest birds and animals, and are correspondingly slighter and less well-developed in those which feed on insects and lizards. There are some notable adaptations for dealing with special prey. The legs of the snake eagles and other species which readily tackle poisonous snakes, are covered in rough, heavy scales as a protection against bites, while the fish-catching specialists, of which the Osprey is the best example, have the undersides of the toes equipped with small, sharp projections known as spicules, which enable them to take and maintain a firm grip on their wet and slippery prey. Birds which spend a good deal of time on the ground, including some of the caracaras, have fairly long legs and relatively blunt claws, while the Secretary Bird has the legs of a fully terrestrial species–long and powerful and quite unlike those of any other member of the Order. At the extreme end of the scale come the vultures with their strong legs and blunt claws–these are birds which almost never kill and must merely be capable of perching and moving with agility on the ground.

While it is the feet which are used more or less exclusively in killing, mention must be made of the bills of the falcons which carry a well-defined 'tooth' on the upper part, used to sever the spinal cord of prey–usually small birds and mammals–which has been captured with the feet. Lizards and other small vertebrates are dealt with similarly by some of the kites, which also have this tooth. The cuckoo-falcons actually bear two such teeth.

Bills vary greatly in size and shape, again in relation to the size and texture of the prey which is eaten. All birds of prey have hooked bills to a greater or lesser degree, the largest and most powerful bills being found on some of the

Left: The long wings and tail of the Marsh Harrier enable it to hunt slowly and methodically

Right: Like all other vultures, the Turkey Vulture can stay aloft for long periods while searching for food and has exceptionally keen eyesight

Below right: The 'fingered' or emarginated flight-feathers of this Red-shouldered Hawk increase the efficiency of the wings during soaring

true eagles, the sea eagles and the big carrion-feeders. Again, some interesting specialization is evident. The Hook-billed Kite of tropical America has a very long, decurved upper mandible which it uses to extract snails from their shells. Precisely how it does this has not been described, but presumably it cannot match the incredible methods of the even more specialized Everglade Kite which, having captured its snail, holds it firmly in one foot and waits patiently until the animal emerges from its shell. It then pierces the soft body with a rapid stab of its long, very finely-curved bill and, as soon as the muscles of the snail relax, flips the shell clear with a single movement.

At the base of the bill, all birds of prey have a bare patch, less horny than the bill itself, called the cere. This is very often yellow in colour and, while the nostrils open into it, its exact function is unknown. A number of birds of prey also have bare lores–the area lying between the base of the bill and the eye. This is a functional development designed to keep this area clean and is often most marked in those species which eat particularly slimy or messy prey. It can be seen well in both the snail-eaters mentioned above, and also in the Black and Crab Hawks

which feed on crabs and similar creatures. A much more extreme development is found in many vultures. Their ugly, naked heads and necks serve a similar purpose and enable them to thrust deep into the flesh and entrails of a carcass and to grub about in such unhygienic situations with a reduced risk of heavily-soiled feathers and the possibility of infection. A quite different development is found in the Honey Buzzard which has the lores covered in short, stiffened feathers which protect it from the stings of bees and wasps as it raids their nests.

Almost all birds have outstandingly good vision, far more acute than our own, and without any doubt it is among the birds of prey that the power of sight has reached its optimum development. Experiments have shown that they have full colour vision. Their very keen perception and ability to distinguish shapes and movement at incredibly long distances come about through special developments in the eye itself. If moving objects are to be judged accurately, it is necessary to be able to adjust the focal length of the lens within the eye, and in raptors the development of the muscles controlling this is more marked than in other birds. Secondly, the retina of the eye shows some extraordinary

modifications. In hawks, the retina of each eye contains two foveae, one of them facing forward and the other sideways. Each fovea is a depression on the retina in which the visual cones are more numerous and concentrated than elsewhere: broadly speaking, the greater the number of cones clustered together, the greater the degree of perception which can be achieved. The forward-facing pair give raptors 'binocular vision' like our own, and all four together produce considerable visual accuracy through an arc of 35 to 50 degrees.

The eyes of birds of prey are large and, especially in those species which dash headlong into thick cover in pursuit of their prey, are rather vulnerable. Birds possess a transparent 'third eyelid' which they can draw across the eye, known as the nictitating membrane. This affords extra protection and also cleans and moistens the eye. It is no doubt brought into play when pursuing and capturing prey in woods or long grass. Many species have a projecting ridge of bone above the eye which must also serve as a protective feature—and it is this feature, incidentally, which creates the impression of a fierce facial expression in so many birds of prey.

While it is the sense of sight that is most important to a hunting bird of prey, hearing is more highly developed than is usually realized. In common with all birds, hawks and their allies hear extremely well and those hunting in woodland and other thick vegetation may well use their ears to some extent in locating prey. None is as highly specialized as the owls, however, some of which are capable of locating and catching prey by ear alone, but at least two groups of raptors have evolved some special features which indicate that hearing is particularly important to them.

The semi-nocturnal forest falcons of the genus *Micrastur* hunt in dense cover, often in very little light; a partial facial ruff formed by a line of small, firm feathers just behind the ear region undoubtedly improves the funnelling of soundwaves towards the ears. Almost owl-like facial ruffs or discs are seen in the *Circus* harriers, and these are even better collectors of sound. In addition, harriers have somewhat larger ear orifices than other hawks; while they hunt mainly in daylight, much of their prey is taken in long grass, reedbeds and so on where it is almost invisible at times. It seems reasonable to conclude from this that harriers can at least detect the presence of prey by sound, even if the final capture also depends on vision.

Birds such as the hobbies may hunt well into the dusk, feeding on flying insects and sometimes bats, but in doing so they rely entirely on their acute eyesight and not on hearing. This is also true of the Bat Hawk, which is more nocturnal than any other bird of prey.

Apart from oddities like the kiwis, which are nocturnal, ground-feeding birds with poor eyesight, most birds cannot smell or have only a very rudimentary sense of smell. This is true of birds of prey—except for the New World vultures, which on anatomical examination are seen to have larger organs of smell than other members of the Order. It is now known that the Turkey Vulture, at least, can locate food partly by smell, although it seems that the American Black Vulture and the two condors cannot.

Above left : Powerful bill of the Golden Eagle—this is used to dismember or tear up the prey and is not used in killing

Above : In contrast, the 'tooth' on the upper mandible of this Peregrine is used to kill prey caught or struck down with the talons

Right : Naked head of a King Vulture—an adaptation allowing the bird to feed on carrion entrails without fouling its feathers

Hunting and Feeding

To many people, it is the process of pursuing and killing other creatures which is the most fascinating aspect of the life of a bird of prey. There are as many fanciful and grossly exaggerated notions of how this happens as there are misunderstandings and misinterpretations of the role of hawks in relation to their prey. Admiration, prejudice and a taste for the sensational rather than the factual combine in the minds of many people to produce some quite fantastic beliefs. Birds of prey are not alone in acquiring an unjustified reputation as ruthless, indiscriminate and spectacular killers: they share the doubtful honour with other misunderstood predators such as lions, crocodiles, sharks and wolves.

At the outset, it is essential that we forget the fabulous massacres of game birds by falcons, the stories of eagles carrying off babies – and all the other tales based on ignorance and prejudice. Instead, we should try and see birds of prey in their role as predators as but one small part in an intricate mosaic of life in which all plants and animals are interdependent. A hawk killing and eating another bird or mammal is no more strange than a spider eating a fly, a cow eating grass or, indeed, a man sitting down to enjoy a fillet steak. We should forget too the idea of 'cruelty', which is a purely human concept practised only by humans: a Peregrine slaying a wild duck does so to eat – not for fun – and it would certainly be wrong to assume that it derives any pleasure from the act. Furthermore, we should understand that birds of prey normally kill only as much as they require to eat – random or wanton killing has no part in their way of life, except in very rare circumstances.

The diurnal birds of prey feed on an astonishingly wide variety of other creatures. Even tiny insects are taken by some, while the largest mammals – elephants and beached whales – are food for others, albeit only as carrion. They are superbly equipped for all kinds of flight and are armed for swift and efficient killing. In this chapter we shall look at the processes of hunting and scavenging and consider the ecological role of birds of prey as predators.

The daily routine of any bird of prey revolves around the need to hunt and eat, whether or not it has a family to feed. Some species make an early start, others which rely on the warmth of the air to produce upcurrents called thermals or activity by their prey do not become active until mid-morning and still others hunt most actively in the evening. Weather, too, has an influence on feeding habits: cold conditions for example, mean that more food is required for survival, and wet weather hinders the activities of many raptors or makes it impossible to hunt.

The size of the prey and the predator are equally important factors. Species which feed on insects or other very small prey will need to spend more time hunting and feeding than birds which can obtain a substantial meal from one source. These considerations relate to the daily requirements of a bird of prey, which may be about 25 per cent of body-weight in a small accipiter but only 7 per cent in a Golden Eagle and perhaps even less in the largest raptors. While a bird like the Hobby must spend many hours each day catching flying insects and an occasional small bird, large eagles and the big vultures and condors can survive for two or three days or more on a single meal. Many birds of

prey have an ability to fast for long periods, and some in captivity have been known to go for as long as two or three weeks without food, suffering no apparent ill-effects in the process.

A single large kill can sustain a big raptor for some days as it may return to an old kill to feed again until nothing is left. Some species, notably the condors and the great vultures, will gorge themselves far beyond their immediate requirements, storing food in their crops. When they are as full as this they may sit around for long periods and can become quite sluggish – though it seems that reports of this making them too heavy to fly off when disturbed have been much exaggerated! A few raptors will even store food in a 'larder' during the breeding season – this habit is well known in the American Kestrel for instance, and among European species, it has also been noted in Eleonora's Falcon.

While large prey is often dismembered and only partly eaten or carried away, smaller items are often swallowed whole. Small mammals may be devoured in one mouthful, though generally speaking this is a more common trait among owls than the diurnal raptors.

The kill is very often taken away to a 'plucking post', rather than being consumed where it was captured. There it is eaten at leisure or parts are selected to be taken to the nest. The external, indigestible parts of birds are discarded, and mammals may be stripped of some of their fur, their feet and so forth. A certain amount of indigestible matter is swallowed, nevertheless, including the bones, the hard parts of beetles and so on, and all this is ejected later from the mouth in a much-compressed, sausage-shaped mass known as a pellet. These pellets may be found at habitual roosts and feeding places, as well as on or around nests. By carefully dissecting them and analyzing their contents it is possible to discover what a particular species is eating. This, and the study of prey remains found at the nest or feeding place comprise the classic methods of studying food intake and prey selection among raptors. Observations at the nest may reveal much about the feeding of the young and often suggest the adult's diet too, but they usually provide only an incomplete picture. Finding out what birds of prey eat by direct observation of their hunting and feeding habits is notoriously difficult with many species and quite impossible with many others.

Although many birds of prey bathe, most drink rarely, if at all. It seems likely that

Above: Indigestible matter is ejected through the mouth in the form of a compact pellet. Dissection and analysis reveal the contents of this Golden Eagle's pellet and enable scientists to form a good idea of its main prey

Right: Securing its food firmly with one foot, a young African Fish Eagle begins feeding

sufficient moisture is obtained from their prey to meet all their needs. Almost the only regular drinkers seem to be the carrion-feeders which often seek water soon after a meal.

In most cases the kill is made using the feet, either by a direct blow or by the immensely powerful grip of the toes together with the deep piercing wounds made by the talons. A number of accounts exist of Peregrines beheading their quarry with the power of their strike, but this is probably exceptional. One example of how talons work shows just how rapid and efficient killing can be in a big, powerful raptor. The author took part in an investigation into the killing of lambs by a pair of Golden Eagles—live lambs are occasionally taken, but much less commonly than is often supposed. One lamb examined had been pierced deeply through the head, neck and shoulders by the spread of one great foot. Any of the wounds could have been mortal, and one talon had gone straight through the animal's shoulder-blade.

Most birds of prey hunt by day; while none are truly nocturnal, there are a few reports of vultures feeding on carcasses by moonlight. Even the Bat Hawk, the most nocturnal, is really a twilight hunter which ceases hunting once the visibility becomes too poor. A number of other species hunt in the evening, chiefly those which

feed on flying insects. In England, the best time of day to watch a European Hobby in action is often towards dusk, and in the Mediterranean region this is true of Eleonora's Falcon and the Red-footed Falcon. Other hawks will hunt small birds which are going to roost. This is particularly true of the small accipiters, and at one major reserve of the Royal Society for the Protection of Birds in England it is almost an evening ritual to watch several Sparrowhawks catching their supper from a vast reedbed roost of Starlings. Birds of prey themselves may be liable to attack while roosting; in Europe, for example, the huge Eagle Owl catches them by night, and even birds as big as Rough-legged Buzzards are not immune.

Sight is the most important sense used while hunting, and the visual acuity of birds of prey is quite outstanding. Highly developed long-range vision is clearly very valuable in locating prey for large, soaring raptors, many of which can spot a possible food source from 2 miles away or more (over 3.2 km), even though they may not hunt from a high altitude. Vultures also rely on their exceptionally keen eyesight in their long, high-flying searches for carrion and in watching the activities of other distant vultures or of other birds and animals which may lead them to a meal.

Species which hunt and kill at high speed, such as some of the large falcons and the accipiters, rely on split-second timing and, very often, the ability to execute astonishing manoeuvres, especially in pursuit of flying prey. These, and the birds which catch flying insects, all show reactions which are closely linked to their superb visual powers.

Although all birds of prey are usually supposed to be highly active, fast-moving aerial hunters, very few are. The majority are relatively slow, patient and inactive birds when searching for prey. Many choose a convenient vantage point, usually well above ground level, where they sit quietly for long periods, scrutinizing the surrounding area for any signs of prey. Depending on the species of raptor and the terrain, these lookout posts may include crags, high rocks, trees or telegraph poles. In woodland, sparrowhawks and goshawks will often sit on the lower branches of trees, immobile but for the constant movements of their heads, while on an open moor a Merlin might use a fence-post, a boulder or even a small hummock in much the same way. From time to time these perches will be changed and the whole process will begin again. A passing bird, or one that

Above : Kestrel hovering. Many birds of prey, especially Kestrels, hover while hunting.

Top left : Gliding Brahminy Kite–ever watchful for likely prey or carrion

Far left : Various remains can be seen on a tree stump 'plucking post' used by this cock European Sparrowhawk

Left : A cock European Sparrowhawk bathing. Most visits to water by birds of prey are for this purpose

a

b

c

Left : This diagram shows
(a) After a short pursuit, a Goshawk may swoop below its victim and seize it as shown
(b) Peregrines kill by striking their prey down from a spectacular, headlong 'stoop'
(c) A circling eagle may descend rapidly and, using a covered approach, take its prey by surprise

Above: Bonelli's Eagle
on a kill. Prey may be
eaten on the spot but is
often carried away to a
favourite feeding-place

appears on the ground or in a tree nearby, will
rouse an accipiter or a Merlin into instant action.
A successful strike is often a very rapid affair
with birds of their speed and adroitness. Sometimes contact is not made and a sustained chase
will ensue. Birds which feed on insects make
short sallies into the air or drop quickly to the
ground, and mammal feeders will launch out
in a slow glide and then strike with a brief burst
of speed. The prey will not infrequently escape
the first attack, and when this happens many
hawks may follow through with a brief pursuit
on the ground.

Roadside fences, poles and wires make excel-
lent bases for hunting operations. Small prey
are often exposed at the roadside, or even on
the road surface, with predictable results, and
passing traffic will flush out other species, especially birds. Much the same principle applies
along railway lines in tropical countries where
small hawks and falcons profit from the commo-
tion of a passing train. Equally, animals and
birds are often killed or maimed by vehicles,
providing ample scope for scavengers and
carrion-feeders such as kites and American
vultures.

In parts of Britain, the Common Buzzard
habitually sits on telegraph poles at the roadside,
and in Scotland probably all the 'Golden Eagles'
seen by tourists just above their passing cars
are Buzzards.

While many birds of prey are capable of short
chases on foot, only a few hunt or forage regularly on the ground. Some of the caracaras and
both the Chanting Goshawks do so, and others
such as the Red Kite and the Common Buzzard
will walk about in fields searching for worms
and large insects. Honey Buzzards regularly find
and attack the nests of bees and wasps on the
ground. The most terrestrial of all raptors is
the Secretary Bird, which spends the greater
part of its day on the ground, striding along
with a deliberate gait at about the walking pace
of a man. At intervals it performs stamping
movements which often disturb or flush out
likely prey. This is then seized and killed with
a quick jab of the bill, although larger prey,
including lizards and snakes, are killed by
stamping.

Many birds of prey hover, notably the various
species of kestrels, the *Elanus* kites, some of the
snake eagles and the Rough-legged Buzzard.
Hovering provides them with an 'aerial perch'
from which they can inspect the area below

them. Many small mammals and probably most insects do not tend to look up, so that attacks from above, either launched from a perch or from a hover, will have a better chance of success than a more direct approach. Hovering, of course, may render a bird of prey more conspicuous to some prey species than using a lookout perch, which is often partly concealed.

The ability to hover might seem to be more efficient than the slow, low-altitude soaring or coursing flight practised by many hunting birds of prey, and yet the latter obviously manage perfectly well. Certainly, many of them will pause to hover briefly, sometimes very clumsily, and even the swiftest hunters will do so from time to time: the author has watched hunting Peregrines hovering, both over coastal marshes

in winter and mountain slopes in the breeding season. Soaring at a great height is often not connected with locating prey, although the vultures are an important exception.

A number of techniques are employed by birds hunting on the wing. Golden Eagles, for example, have been observed killing birds in full flight, even at great heights above the ground, and they will sometimes kill in a tremendous power-dive from above, reaching speeds of 100 miles per hour (about 160 km/h). Their more normal mode of hunting, however, is more dogged, and exemplifies one of the most common methods used by raptors. The essence of the technique is persistence and thoroughness, with the ever-present possibility of surprise. The bird may, for example, spend some time gliding

Above : Augur Buzzard pouncing on a lizard. Many species take their prey on the ground, either by a direct strike or after a short chase on foot

Above : A falconer's Peregrine 'mantling' its prey with its wings in a manner common to many birds of prey

quite rapidly over likely terrain, hoping to surprise likely prey such as grouse or hares, which are momentarily exposed. If the prey is sighted, a brief burst of speed is followed by a lightning strike.

Whilst hunting in this way a Golden Eagle may be chased and harried by smaller birds, such as Hooded Crows, as it flies through their territory. Such activity rarely causes the eagle to change direction, apart from an occasional sideslip – but it may alert possible prey. Grouse, for example, often take off in a panic on seeing a Golden Eagle. It is interesting to note that without the advantage of altitude a Golden Eagle cannot match the pace of grouse in level flight.

Sometimes the eagle may glide more slowly, close to the ground, angling around large rocks and occasionally slipping along gullies. Steering by small movements of its tail and wing-tips, and occasionally maintaining forward momentum with several deep flaps, it covers large areas of ground at a steady speed, searching thoroughly. Perhaps half an hour of this careful, relentless hunting may pass before an opportunity arises, and even then if unsuccessful, the eagle may well hunt on for hours.

Harriers, too, hunt low down, usually travelling rather slowly, coursing over all sorts of open terrain, ceaselessly searching and probably listening too. Their flight is more buoyant and erratic than that of many larger raptors. There are often changes of direction, long glides and occasional brief bursts of speed or spells of hovering. Because their prey is mostly very small and often almost invisible, hunting is a prolonged affair, probably involving a number of kills each day and more when they have a family to feed. There are few things as satisfying to an observer as watching these graceful, long-winged birds at work, especially on windy days.

For the most part it is the combination of continuous flying and low airspeed and altitude which enables a harrier to be such an efficient hunter. The bigger Bateleur Eagle, so much a feature of the African sky, is also an aerial hunter which courses to and fro over large areas for hours on end—but this bird does so at speeds of up to 40 miles per hour (64 km/h), and seems to compensate for impaired vision at this speed by flying at a much greater height above ground than most harriers.

Species which catch flying insects have exceptionally acute perception and great dexterity. Birds such as the hobbies will often hunt and feed continuously where large insects are numerous, taking the prey in their feet and holding it up to their bills so that they actually eat while flying along. On a warm summer evening in England, the author and some colleagues watched a European Hobby feeding on Summer Chafers, large, rotund insects which were thick in the air above a cornfield. The bird cruised up and down, 30 to 40 feet (9 to 12 m) up, taking prey in one foot at regular intervals. For 23 minutes it caught and ate chafers at an approximate rate of one every 15 seconds, and thus must have accounted for about 100 during this single spell of feeding.

The European Hobby and several closely related falcons are among the most rapid fliers of all birds of prey, and all are adept at catching other birds in full flight. Although they often use surprise and make full use of altitude to gain an advantage in speed, they are also able to outfly most birds in level flight and have great manoeuvrability. Even such superb fliers as swifts and swallows are not safe when a European Hobby comes among them. The Merlin, too, is an amazing flier when bird-hunting, but without any doubt the Peregrine is the bird hunter *par excellence*. Although it cannot outfly a healthy grouse, a Golden Plover or even an ordinary pigeon in a level chase, it kills many of these birds. It relies on height when hunting, killing with extraordinary skill and accuracy from a stupendous dive or 'stoop' in which it may well achieve speeds of around 200 miles per hour (320 km/h). On moorland, it is interesting to compare the reactions of grouse to hunting eagles and Peregrines: the grouse is often able to escape from an eagle if it flies, but will tend to stay on the ground when a Peregrine is near.

Below: An adult Bald Eagle feeding on a fish. This species is quite capable of capturing fish and other live prey but will also scavenge and feed on a wide variety of carrion

Raptors which hunt in woodland and forest commonly use perches, making brief sallies and short surprise attacks from them. This general rule applies as much to the forest falcons and the small accipiters as to the huge but similarly shaped Harpy and Monkey-eating Eagles. Another hunting method is to fly through a wood, weaving in and out of the trees, using all the available cover and launching sudden attacks from full flight. Most of the small sparrowhawks regularly hunt in this way, through woods and along hedgerows, even flying among buildings and gardens. Their use of cover and 'dead ground' is often remarkable, and it is highly characteristic of a hunting sparrowhawk to rush repeatedly – and furiously – down one side of a hedge, hop over the top, dash down the other side, and then hop back again. The author followed a bird hunting down a stretch of road in Wales where it was using exactly this technique, and timed it on a car speedometer at 40 miles per hour (64 km/h). Surprise is their chief weapon, allied with speed and great agility, but they will often pursue other birds in the open with great persistence and are fully capable of flying down all but the swiftest of them.

The boldness of sparrowhawks when hunting is well known. They will ignore people and animals and not infrequently enter buildings if their quarry seeks refuge there. Collisions with windows are commonly reported, and there have even been stories of sparrowhawks becoming inextricably entangled in hedges and other thick vegetation as they dash headlong after their escaping prey. Some sparrowhawks take small mammals as readily as they do birds. In North America, for instance, Cooper's Hawk will watch and wait until a squirrel or chipmunk is in the open before launching a rapid, surprise attack from a perch. Very similar methods are employed, against mammals and birds alike, by goshawks in Europe, North America and Australia. Cooper's Hawk is remarkably adept at catching bats in full flight, despite the considerable speed and agility of these rather strange, flying mammals.

A number of hawks are experts at taking prey from water. Undoubtedly, the Osprey is the master fisherman among birds of prey, though many of the sea eagles, the African Fish Eagle in particular, the two Fishing Eagles from Asia and the Fishing Buzzard are specialists in this field. Most of them hunt from the air or from a perch above or near the water, and expertly

lift fish swimming close to the surface with one foot. The Fishing Buzzard and Fish Eagles, however, may plunge right in after prey.

The Osprey may also hunt from a perch. More often it soars in circles up to 100 feet (30 m) above the water, peering intently downwards and sometimes pausing to hover rather clumsily. When a fish is sighted, the bird executes a spectacular headlong plunge after it, at the last moment bringing the feet forward beneath and in front of the head to strike. An Osprey will often enter the water with a considerable splash, but it is soon airborne again and quickly moves the fish into a fore-and-aft position in the feet, reminiscent of a torpedo being carried underneath an aeroplane. When it is well clear of the water, and before it sets off towards its nest

or feeding place, it characteristically pauses in mid-air and briskly shakes clear the surplus water from its plumage.

The White-bellied Sea Eagle, besides being a thoroughly competent fisherman, has a speciality of its own. Sea-snakes are common from India south-east to Australasia, and form a major part of its diet; they are taken from the surface of the water as they come up to breathe.

The big sea eagles will not miss an opportunity to attack and kill birds swimming on the water, especially if they show any signs of weakness or disability. White-tailed Eagles, for example, will harry divers and other birds, causing them to dive repeatedly to escape, and will maintain this so incessantly that the wretched victim, exhausted, becomes an easy kill. A pair of eagles

Above: Rüppell's Griffons squabbling at a carcass: individuals establish dominance according to their hunger and may not leave a kill until they are gorged

may do this together, giving their quarry even less chance of escape. Similar tactics are employed by Bald Eagles in America. It is quite common for a pair of raptors to share a kill made by one of them, but close co-operation in the hunting task is much more unusual.

Klepto-parasitism, or the stealing of food from another animal in preference to capturing prey, is well known among several families of birds, yet piracy of this kind is relatively uncommon among birds of prey. Its chief exponents are the more omnivorous or scavenging species, notably some of the kites and sea eagles. The Bald Eagle, a large and powerful member of the genus *Haliaeetus*, has a reputation as a robber of Ospreys. The eagle chases and harries the smaller bird relentlessly until it is forced

to drop its catch, which the eagle then retrieves in mid-air. Bald Eagles have also been known to bully vultures sufficiently to make them disgorge a recently swallowed meal. Other species use piratical tactics occasionally, and perhaps a few individuals develop them as a habit. The European Kestrel seems an unlikely bandit, but the author has seen one pursue a Barn Owl which had been hunting in broad daylight and wrest a vole from the owl's talons with very little difficulty.

Since the earliest known bird of prey, *Lith-ornis*, was a vulturine type, probably with habits very similar to those of the New World vultures, it is reasonable to suppose that all the species we know today have evolved from scavengers and carrion-feeders. Certainly many of the

species regarded as the most primitive in form scavenge or eat carrion, either partly or exclusively. The habit has not been lost among some species which occupy a higher position on the evolutionary ladder. In the genus *Aquila*, for example, we find the Golden Eagle frequently resorting to carrion when natural prey is scarce, and its close cousin the Tawny Eagle is also known as a scavenger. Any vaguely edible material, animal or vegetable, may be eaten by the smaller vultures and species such as the Black and Brahminy Kites. Scavengers like these often live in close association with primitive human communities and may rely on human refuse as a major food source in some regions.

We tend to take for granted the collection and disposal of refuse in Western societies. We are not used to seeing dead domestic animals and decaying garbage left to rot. In some regions, especially in parts of the tropics, all this is perfectly normal and it cannot be stressed too strongly that, whatever our instinctive revulsion towards them, the scavenging birds of prey (and with them the hyenas, jackals, Marabou Storks and so on) play an important and beneficial role in helping to eliminate waste and minimize the spread of disease.

Vultures are quick to find a carcass, either by their own direct observation or by watching the behaviour of other distant vultures, other carrion-feeding birds and various scavenging animals. They plane in at considerable speed, often from great heights and long distances, and frequently congregate at a dead body in large numbers, sitting around in groups and, depending on their hunger, assuming a temporary dominance over their neighbours as they go in to feed. At other times, many will feed together in a noisy jostling mass. Even the bodies of large animals will be reduced to mere bones in the space of an hour or two, or even less.

The largest and most powerful species, the Black and Lappet-faced Vultures, will dominate the Griffons and other Old World species at a carcass and when they arrive late—as they often do—they are quite capable of driving other large vultures away so that they can feed. Breaking into a carcass is often a lengthy business, even for the biggest vultures, and kills left partly eaten by big predators are clearly an easier proposition. Once an inroad has been made, however, progress is swift. Their long naked necks are thrust well into the body cavity of dead animals and they may even go right inside to feed.

Above : The Black-breasted Harrier Eagle like many snake eagles, swallows small prey whole

Above right : Contrary to popular belief, even true eagles like this Tawny Eagle may eat carrion

Right : Immature Egyptian Vulture about to drop a stone onto an egg to break the shell

Overleaf : Hunting African Fish Eagle, pulled into the water by the weight of the fish

The smaller, weaker-billed species, and also the Lammergeier (not a dominant or aggressive bird, despite its great size) must wait until the bigger vultures have begun their grisly work before they can join in. They remain around the fringes, picking up small morsels, until the bigger birds move away, when they, with the other small scavengers such as kites and ravens, take over to finish the corpse.

Vultures can see off many smaller scavengers easily, but the big Marabou Stork is powerful enough to compete with them and mammals such as hyenas and wolves can drive vultures away from a carcass.

The Lammergeier or Bearded Vulture is remarkable for one peculiar habit, recorded in literature of ancient times but only confirmed recently. It will carry off large bones and drop them onto rocks from heights of up to 200 feet (60 m), smashing them open to obtain the marrow inside. The manoeuvre is carried out while flying downwind, the bird turning rapidly into the wind after the drop so that it can pull up immediately and drop down to the bone before the arrival of any other scavengers which might have been following the flying Lammergeier very closely.

71

The role of birds of prey in relation to their food supply has been misrepresented and misunderstood. In general, there is an equilibrium in nature between the hunters and the hunted: a predator does not exterminate its food supply or – except in local or purely temporary circumstances – have any effect on the numbers of any of its prey species. In any species, a surplus of individuals is produced over and above the numbers required to maintain its population. This surplus is reduced through disease, inability to find a suitable habitat in which to live and feed, predation and other mortality factors. Birds of prey crop part of this surplus. While it is often said that raptors control the numbers of their prey, the reverse is in fact the case: the state of a bird of prey population – its numbers, breeding success and so on – is dependent upon the availability of food.

Scottish Golden Eagles are a good example. These big, rapacious birds have been studied in detail over the last three decades. In spite of this, there are still many misconceptions about them and their position in relation to livestock and game birds.

The home range of a pair of eagles in Scotland is between 20 and 28 square miles (5,178 and 7,250 ha). This area must provide enough food each year for two breeding adults, an average

of less than one youngster reared by them each year and, in addition, one or two unattached adults or immature birds which may also be present. It has been calculated from detailed studies that the annual food requirement of all these birds in a home range is a little more than 1,000 lbs (450 kg), and in areas studied so far it seems that the total amount of prey and carrion available (excluding abnormal prey, to which the birds will turn if pressed) is 10 to 20 times greater than this. Thus it will be evident that a home range contains a superabundance of prey and that the eagles' effect on it in terms of numbers is very slight indeed. While work on other species in other countries, notably in the United States, shows that immigrant birds of prey may limit the numbers of prey species in some areas in winter, the effects are not marked enough to alter the basic annual pattern. Studies of most species carried out to date show broadly similar results to those obtained for Scottish Golden Eagles.

In Scotland, about 25 to 30 per cent of the eagles' prey consists of birds. The Red Grouse, a popular game bird weighing only about 20 ounces (566 g), is a favoured prey of the big birds. Yet it is nonsense to claim, as many will, that eagles kill enormous numbers of them. On average, a Golden Eagle requires to eat only

Above: Osprey feeding young – even quite large chicks may be fed by their parents for some time before they are able to cope themselves

7 per cent of its own body weight of about 8 or 10 pounds (3·6 or 4·5 kg) each day to maintain itself – and it will not kill more prey than it needs. Even allowing for a wastage factor of around 20 per cent in each grouse killed, the numbers actually taken are far below those commonly claimed by game-keepers. The author was assured by one keeper that the local eagles killed 20 to 30 grouse every week, which was clearly absurd. Furthermore, detailed studies of grouse populations in Scotland have shown that predation by eagles, foxes and other predators does not account for more than 7 per cent of the annual mortality rate. Some slightly different results have been obtained from other studies of birds of prey and game birds, but none of these shows that the raptor in question is seriously influencing the numbers of its prey.

In western Scotland especially, eagles breed in sheep country where, owing to the very presence of these animals, natural prey is scarce, and here carrion forms an important source of food, especially in winter. It is quite untrue to claim that eagles never kill lambs – they do, but only rarely and then only when the lambs are very small or sickly. The great majority of lambs brought in to eyries (and some eagles may bring in quite a lot) are picked up dead and the heavy mortality among young hill sheep is not caused by predation but by a system of land-use which badly needs reforming. Similar conclusions have been drawn from other studies made of birds of prey in relation to livestock. Their predation is usually negligible, except in certain situations where, for one reason or another, man has made his stock particularly vulnerable. The solution is almost always to improve conditions for the livestock, not ruthlessly to shoot and trap the predators.

There is really no case for regarding Golden Eagles as 'vermin'. Their continued persecution by some keepers and shepherds in Scotland is no more justified than the incredible campaigns waged with aeroplanes and marksmen against the same species in the western United States, the slaughter of Wedge-tailed Eagles by Australian farmers, or the widespread trapping of goshawks and sparrowhawks. Much of the work on birds of prey indicates that they have been misunderstood. Very few are ever in conflict with man's interests, many are beneficial and most are neutral. However, as we shall see in the final chapter of this book, convincing people of this is another matter.

The Breeding Cycle

Left : The nest of the Shikra, a sparrowhawk of the savannahs of Africa, India and southern Asia

Before outlining the processes of courtship and breeding, it is necessary to discuss the defined areas in which birds of prey live – their territories, or, more appropriately in this Order of birds, their home ranges.

Many kinds of birds are markedly territorial and this is of great importance with regard to their breeding behaviour. A territory is an area in which a bird nests and feeds, to the exclusion of others of the same species. It may be vigorously defended, with song posts from which the owner advertises his presence against closely related or even wholly different species. Certain forms of territory exist outside the breeding season in both resident and migratory birds. Other birds, especially those that breed in colonies, may not be territorial at all, except in the immediate area of their nests, and may share feeding areas with neighbours and with other species.

Most birds of prey are strongly territorial only around their nest sites, and will share hunting areas with others of the same species. It is usual to call their whole area of operation their home range, rather than their territory, since the latter implies that they defend the whole area. A few species, such as some North American members of the genus *Buteo*, may defend a favoured 'hunting territory' within their home range, as well as their actual nest territory, but this is quite unusual.

Territorialism varies greatly among the raptors. While most are solitary birds during the breeding season, some are most gregarious and breed in colonies; notable examples are some of the kites and Old World vultures, African Fish Eagles, Ospreys and falcons like Eleonora's, the Red-footed and the Lesser Kestrel. While these birds will defend a very small area immediately around their own nests they will use common hunting grounds and also feed in parties. At the other end of the spectrum we find a species such as the Prairie Falcon which may defend the entire home range. This is not unknown with other species but only occurs rarely, in areas where the home range is particularly small.

Most species – whatever the size of their home range (which may be less than half a square mile (129 ha) in many small hawks and falcons or 30 square miles (7,767 ha) in some large eagles) – will tolerate members of their own and other raptor species and share hunting grounds. Two or three pairs of Peregrines or Golden Eagles, for example, may have overlapping home ranges where they are not aggressive to one another – although around the nesting cliff they will be most possessive and drive off any intruders.

We have said that the availability of food is a major factor governing the populations of birds of prey. The home range is a limiting factor too, and not only in the context of furnishing enough prey. The availability of suitable nest sites is vital and spatial distribution is also important as non-colonial raptors will not nest close to one another.

Birds of prey have no song with which to announce ownership of the area which they defend against others of the same species – nor do most have extensive 'advertisement displays' to perform the same function, although the frequent habit of soaring above the nesting area – so obvious in a number of species – may have the same role.

Intruders are generally chased off, often very vigorously, although actual physical contact is the exception rather than the rule. Other birds of prey will be harassed too, whether they are larger or smaller species, as will most potential bird or animal predators, including dogs, foxes and leopards. Relatively few raptors will attack a human being, however. It is worth mentioning that birds of prey are in their turn 'mobbed' by other, non-predatory birds, irrespective of size differences—indeed this must be an everyday experience for many of them. By drawing attention to possible predators, many small birds can increase their own chances of survival, surprisingly enough just by making a nuisance of themselves. Retaliation by birds of prey is not unknown, but it is quite unusual. It is a common sight to see any small falcon or accipiter harried by song-birds, buzzards worried by crows and gulls, or eagles being chased by other smaller birds.

Courtship displays assume great importance with the onset of the breeding season. Sometimes they begin in winter quarters or during the homeward flights of migrant birds of prey. With sedentary species the displays may commence on fine days in late winter. In birds which pair for life, such as the Golden Eagle, courtship display provides the necessary stimulus for mating as well as strengthening the pair bond. Other species, such as many of the smaller hawks, also use it to advertise for a mate. Even after the eggs are laid, or the young well grown, these displays may continue at a lower intensity than in spring, and are clearly important in maintaining ties between a pair. Most display is performed by the male bird, but it may be carried out to a lesser extent by the females of some species.

While birds of prey have no song and largely lack the often exotic breeding plumage of other birds, their displays are often incredibly spectacular, especially among those species which perform them in the air. Many of the forest-dwelling species, such as the sparrowhawks and goshawks, may emulate the advertisement display of song-birds by choosing a conspicuous perch from which they call continuously; others, including the accipiters, many of the *Buteo* hawks and some falcons, soar and call high above their territories. These tactics usually announce the presence of a male bird and attract possible mates to him, but they may continue beyond the pairing stage or be performed by a pair of birds together.

A great many raptors have wonderful aerial courtship displays. Often these take place very high above the territory and may be performed over a wide area. Shallow, undulating flights, for example, are seen in many accipiters and, like the smaller falcons, they will often stoop almost vertically downwards for hundreds of feet, pulling up to regain height and recommence. Incredibly steep, spectacular undulations are performed by many of the falcons and buzzards and, most impressively, by the large *Aquila* eagles and even the Secretary Bird. These birds may plunge downwards for hundreds of feet, sweeping up to regain their original height and repeating the process again and again. Some, like the Tawny Eagle, descend by stages, using steep dives and shorter upward swings. In many of these undulating displays it is not uncommon for birds to roll onto their backs briefly—the

Marsh Harrier has been said to have looped-the-loop on occasion. Verreaux's Eagle has another variation–diving, regaining height and then swinging back to repeat the manoeuvre in the opposite direction. It does this again and again, performing figures-of-eight high in the sky.

The Honey Buzzard has a singularly attractive display by which it can be identified at great distances. It will pause while soaring to clap its wings together high above its back. Other birds will soar close together in a form of mutual display–this can be seen in some of the Old World vultures–and many of the large, soaring eagles and buzzards will touch talons in flight. The female will roll onto her back, touch the pendant talons of the male descending above her, and right herself in an instant. Some of

the huge sea eagles actually lock talons and, with wings held high above their backs, cartwheel crazily downwards for hundreds of feet before parting.

While these displays are spectacular and highly stimulating to the birds concerned, they may not necessarily be a prerequisite of mating which, among many larger species at least, often takes place with no apparent preliminaries. Some pre-mating displays do occur, however. Male falcons will 'courtship-feed' their mates first (this is common among many Orders of birds) and a number of accipiters have wild, twisting courtship chases beforehand.

Although male raptors, such as Peregrines and some of the bird-hawks, may take part in prospecting, studies suggest that final selection of

Above : Egyptian Vultures mating. The act of copulation may or may not be preceded by courtship displays

the nest-site rests with the female. In many species which build nests or repair old ones, it is the female who does most of the building. In many species, however, the male assists in collecting nest material and in some, including the Osprey and some of the kites, he may bring in most of it. Sticks of various sizes are usually the basic material, but where these are not available other matter, such as heather stems or seaweed, is used. Smaller, finer vegetation—grass, rushes, or moss—often lines the main structure. Some species, especially among the kites, often use paper or rubbish as part of the nest material, sometimes providing the home with a surprising splash of colour. Of course, some species make no nest at all and lay their eggs on a bare ledge or make a mere scrape in the ground.

Some birds of prey build a new nest each year—many of the goshawks and sparrowhawks are examples—and some, such as the buzzards and the Osprey, simply repair a site used in the previous year. Still others, like the Golden Eagle, may have a number of nests and will use them alternately or in approximate rotation, often making repairs to two or three nests before lining the one finally used. As a general rule, it can be said that the bigger the bird of prey, the less likely it is to build an entirely fresh nest. Another rather general rule is that the further north, the more rapidly the nests are built. This is due to the shortness of the breeding season in high latitudes—construction can proceed more slowly in the tropics where the pressure of time upon birds is less.

Above: Martial Eagles at the nest. The female (right) has brought in a fresh green spray—the reason for this behaviour is probably connected with excitement and not with nest sanitation, as has often been suggested

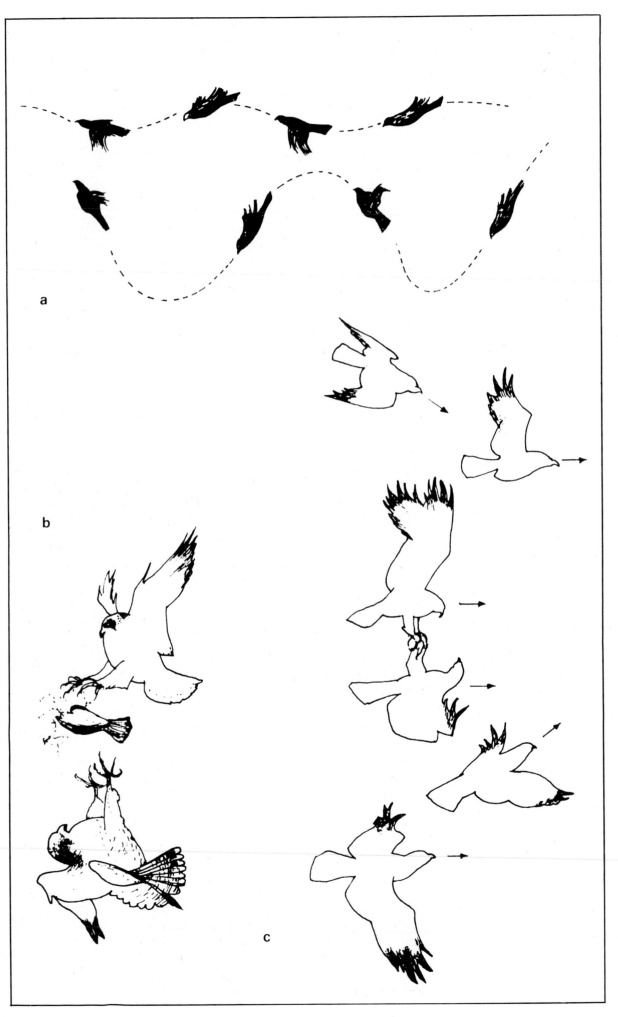

Left : This diagram
shows
(a) Two forms of
undulating display
flight used by many
birds of prey
(b) 'Food passes' occur
during courtship and
feeding of the young :
the male drops the prey
and the female rolls over
to receive it in her talons
(c) One of the most
spectacular courtship
displays is found in the
huge sea eagles—the
male descends to meet
the female, they lock
claws and cartwheel
downwards before
parting

a

b

c

Some raptors, notably the true falcons, will take over the nests of other birds. The Red-footed Falcon, for example, will use old rooks' nests, and European Hobbies those of crows. These may be taken over as they stand or may be rebuilt or added to. The largest falcons, such as Peregrines, Lanners and Gyrs, may even usurp a nest and drive off its owner. Oddly enough, in some cases the lower part of a raptor's nest may be inhabited by other birds: various kinds of small birds have been found in the 'basements' of nests belonging to Swainson's Hawks in the United States; while in Africa several species have had weaver-birds as tenants. Curiously, these small neighbours are usually tolerated or treated with indifference by the raptors.

Not all birds of prey nest on steep, inaccessible cliffs and crags – though some certainly do. The author has seen Golden Eagles' eyries which only a skilled mountaineer could reach and others one could almost drive into. Most species nest in trees, usually well above the ground. Accipiters, buzzards and various others tend to build in a big fork or where a thick branch joins the trunk, but some, such as the Osprey and various eagles, nest on the exposed crown. Relatively few species use cliffs and crags and even fewer nest on the ground. In some species the

choice of site depends on what is available. Peregrines are traditionally cliff-nesters, but use trees in some regions (Poland, for example), and in the Arctic may nest more or less on the ground. Similarly, the Osprey, characteristically a tree-nester, is found on cliffs near the Mediterranean and on the ground in America and Australia. While some Golden Eagles nest only on crags or cliffs, others use trees – but some pairs have alternate sites of both kinds.

Artificial sites, provided by man, have been used by some species. Ospreys have nested on poles topped with cartwheels in America, and in Europe nestboxes of several sorts have been used by Kestrels. Nesting in or on buildings is not uncommon among species habitually frequenting towns – Kestrels again are good examples and perhaps the most famous were the Peregrines which nested regularly on the ledge of a building high above New York some years ago.

In addition to the normal process of lining their nests, some birds of prey have the attractive habit of decorating them with fresh greenery. This is most prevalent before the eggs are laid but often continues throughout the breeding cycle. It seems that this behaviour may be connected with excitement, but the reasons for it are hard to determine. It has been suggested

Below : In the courtship display of the Andean Condor, the male (left) tiptoes around the smaller female with wings spread and head bowed towards her. She adopts a crouching posture

that these sprays of leaves or other vegetation may be used to shelter the young or to cover the decaying and often fly-infested prey remains which are so often a feature of nests in which young are growing up – but observations do not support these theories and any such use seems to be incidental. Unfortunately, we must rule out the aesthetic feelings of the birds towards the attractiveness of their homes – a common theory it would be nice to believe!

While there is a good deal of variation in bird of prey eggs, most conform to a fairly basic pattern, having a basic or ground colour of white, (sometimes bluish or greenish) either unmarked or marked with red, brown or grey. Falcons' eggs are rather different. They usually have dense spotting or clouding, with red markings,

and sometimes the mottling is so heavy that it almost hides the whitish or buff ground-colour. Most eggs are rounded rather than elongated and are relatively large in comparison to the size of the bird.

The raptors usually lay small clutches of eggs: one to three eggs are most usual, four or five being uncommon. None of the really large species lays more than three eggs and generally the largest clutches are laid by the smallest birds. Another general rule, common to many birds, applies within the Order – the clutch size of a species tends to increase the farther north it occurs. This is in accordance with the theory that more northerly populations may have higher post-fledging mortality rates than those further south.

Above left:
Sparrowhawk's nest

Right: Verreaux's
Eagle in a typical crag
site. In common with
other eagles and many
large raptors, this
species builds a large
and bulky nest

The eggs are laid at intervals of at least one day apart and often the spacing may be as much as three or more days. This results in asynchronous hatching and a considerable size discrepancy is obvious between brothers and sisters in the same nest. The larger, earlier-born chicks thus begin life with a distinctly better chance of survival.

The incubation period is a long one, being around three weeks in the smallest species and up to 50 days or even more in the largest ones – though accurate data on incubation periods are lacking for most birds of prey. The female takes the greater share in sitting, and towards the time of hatching will become noticeably reluctant to leave the eggs. Males share incubation duties to some extent in some species, especially when the female leaves the nest to feed after he has brought in prey for her. During incubation, females seem to show little interest in killing and will often sit for hours watching potential prey around or below them without moving in the slightest.

At first, raptor chicks are helpless little creatures, big-headed, weak-legged and largely immobile as they lie in their coats of first down. They cannot take food until they are strong enough to reach up to the parent's bill for it and with some species chicks may not feed at

Left : European Hobby with young. Hobbies characteristically use the old nests of crows and other birds

Below : Relatively few birds of prey nest on the ground, but Marsh Harriers always do so, usually in dense reedbeds or long grass

all until they are at least a day old. But as their strength increases so does their appetite and before they leave the nest altogether they will have increased their original hatching weight by about 50 times.

Because hatching is often at intervals of several days the rates of development differ between members of the same brood. When food is in good supply, this is of no importance, but in some species, notably the *Aquila* eagles, this size difference between two chicks produces a curious phenomenon generally known as the 'Cain and Abel battle': the elder chick consistently attacks the younger one and, in about 80 per cent of the cases studied, kills it or pitches it out of the nest–to a certain death. Even if she happens to be on the nest while this is happening, the female parent does not intervene. The critical period for the younger chick is the first week or so of its life. If it manages to survive that period and to obtain enough food the danger quickly passes and it is left alone. This grim struggle for survival is not properly understood, although it may be related to the availability of food. The bigger, more vigorous youngster will always be fed first and only when there is sufficient food for the smaller chick to eat

its fill after the first is sated will both be likely to survive.

Soon, a second, thicker and 'woollier' coat of down replaces the first, making the young bird less susceptible to cold and wet. The hen bird broods her young less and less often as they grow in size and competence, although while they are relatively small she will still do so in adverse weather and at night–and, equally, she will often shade them from the full force of the sun. As the youngsters grow up, their mother spends less and less time on the nest with them, although she is seldom far away. She defends her young readily against predators (and indeed the young themselves will put on a good show of defiance when threatened). Despite their reputation for ferocity, very few birds of prey will attack a human being at the nest. Some will use a good deal of threatening behaviour and a few, like the Northern Goshawk and the Hen Harrier, may even strike–but many just fly off or protest from a distance. The Golden Eagle, popularly supposed to knock men off cliffs, will almost never come near a man, let alone mount a determined attack on him.

The first feathers to appear are those of the wings and tail, which become easy to perceive

about one-third to two-fifths of the way through the fledging period. These are followed by the body feathers, with those of the upper parts usually developing more quickly than those below. By this stage, young raptors are big and confident, standing and walking in the nest and exercising their stumpy wings vigorously. Even before they are fully feathered they are able to feed themselves on the prey left on the nest by their parents. Begging for food, so much a feature of their earliest days, is replaced by an almost aggressive attitude towards their parents.

Throughout the fledging period, the care given to the young by their parents, especially the female, is quite remarkable. The male's main function is hunting during the period when the female cannot safely leave the young, and his

Above: Kestrels often nest in buildings and take readily to artificial sites

Left: In this Hen Harrier's nest, asynchronous hatching is shown particularly well—both small chicks and unhatched eggs can be seen

visits to the nest are usually fleeting. Even so, the males of some species assist in feeding the young and cases have been reported of them bringing up the young alone after the loss of the female. The male may bring the prey to the nest whole, or in pieces, plucked or unplucked, but may call the female off to receive food. In the harriers, the female flies up to meet the male in mid-air and there is a spectacular food-pass, the male dropping the prey for the female to catch.

Young raptors leave the nest at varying ages, according to the size of the species and the rate of their development. The young of the smaller falcons and hawks may fledge at 3 or 4 weeks of age, but the period is much longer in the larger species—it may be 10 to 13 weeks in large

eagles and as long as 5 months in the great condors. Once again, fledging periods tend to be longer in the tropics than for similar species further north, again relating to the much shorter time available for the breeding cycle in northern latitudes.

The first flight may be a clumsy affair in which the youngster may not travel far, or on the other hand it may take the new raptor a long way from its first home. Young birds of prey are often dependent on their parents for food for a long time, even after they can fly well. They possess an innate instinct to kill, but must learn from their parents and from constant practice how to do it properly and efficiently. Their first attempts to secure prey can be clumsy and, to the observer, hilarious.

The smaller species become independent fairly quickly, as do many migratory species such as the Osprey. In very large species, especially some of the tropical eagles, the period of dependence on the adults may be very long. For instance, the Crowned Eagle in equatorial Africa is with its parents for so long that they breed only every other year. A similar situation is believed to exist with the big Harpy Eagle in South America, and no doubt does so with other species.

In due course the young disperse, often in a seemingly random way, although they are not driven away by their parents as is commonly supposed. Immature birds must find areas where they can kill enough prey to support themselves but in some species they may well share part of their parents' home range for some time after becoming independent. We know relatively little about this stage of their lives, but it is certain that it is a critical period. During their first year on their own, mortality is very high–probably at least 50 per cent.

How breeding success or productivity relates to the survival of a species is only partly understood. Few birds of prey have been studied in sufficient depth for us to understand how their population dynamics work. In simple terms, for a species to maintain its numbers, the number of young reaching maturity must be sufficient to replace the adults which die. Clutch sizes, the rate of hatching (infertile eggs are not uncommon in some raptors) and the fact that apparently healthy birds do not breed in some years are all factors which affect the production of young. We should also consider other issues, such as the very slow rate of reproduction of some of the larger species, or how productivity might be affected by bigamy–among harriers bigamy is not uncommon and usually results in fewer young reared per nest than in normal situations. Taking such factors into account we can arrive at a reasonable figure for fledging success for any species, but then comes the difficult question of finding out how many birds reach adulthood. We know that in their first year many youngsters perish and have said already that around 50 per cent might do so–in some of the larger species it is estimated to be as high as 75 per cent. In some species mortality rates decrease as these young birds get older and become more experienced. The process of reaching maturity may be quite a long one, four or five years in the big *Aquila* eagles, for example, and as long as eight or nine years in the two condors.

Much data and intensive studies are required to make calculations of the numbers of young

Below : Black–shouldered Kites from Australia. In the first weeks of life, young birds receive constant and devoted attention

Above: Wahlberg's Eagle and young. It is impossible not to be impressed by the care with which these large raptors tend their young

per annum which will survive to replace adults, and, in the case of many birds of prey, this information is often not available. Nevertheless, we are able to make some tentative assumptions and, for some species, to make an intelligent guess: for example, it has been estimated that only one out of every five Golden Eagles born each year survives to reach adulthood. This means that a pair which breed every year would take ten years to replace themselves. Smaller raptors have shorter lives and greater annual productivity, while some of the very large tropical eagles might take 20 years to replace themselves.

It is difficult to assess the length of birds' lives. Even with a number of population studies and helpful results from the recovery of ringed birds we can only guess with most species, but small garden birds often have an average life-span of a year or even less. Larger species tend to mature more slowly and to live longer and this basic rule seems to apply to the birds of prey.

In the wild, it is improbable that the smaller species of hawks and falcons ever survive beyond 10 years of age. Among the larger vultures and eagles, however, it is quite likely that they may reach or exceed 20 years on average, their longevity compensating for their long period of immaturity and their low annual rate of breeding productivity. There are, of course, many records for captive birds of prey and among the larger species ages of 30 to 40 years are common. Some have lived to 50 and beyond, but the popular belief that eagles and vultures can become centenarians is quite unfounded: no well-documented records exist of even a captive bird approaching that age.

It is the availability of food which ultimately controls numbers. This is a factor controlling breeding success and the mortality of adults and immature birds alike. Death may come through disease, predation, accidents, or old age, all of which are 'natural' factors. What has been called by some 'the balance of nature', allows for this and normally birds of prey rear enough young to sustain and sometimes even to increase their numbers. Short-term natural catastrophes may alter the situation slightly or temporarily but, only man, the super-predator, has the ability to change this delicate balance critically and permanently. Without any doubt, it is man who exerts the greatest influence over the mortality and survival of many raptors.

Migration

Migration is a favourite topic among ornithologists, and the subject has been widely studied in North America and Western Europe. Much remains, however, to be discovered about the migrations which take place in Asia and other regions.

Broadly speaking, migration is the movement of certain birds to and from areas in which they live at different seasons. Migratory species breed in one area, using optimum conditions for the vital, energy-sapping business of rearing their young, and then move elsewhere to find the best conditions for the non-breeding season. These movements are not undertaken simply because of weather conditions but rather in response to the availability of food—although obviously the two factors are closely interrelated. Migration may be purely local (even from one altitude to another) or from one country to another; very commonly it is intercontinental.

Several factors may complicate the issue. In some species of birds of prey, only part of the population may migrate, either in terms of geographical distribution or of age-groups. Equally, migrant birds may occur alongside resident breeding birds of the same species—a very complex situation arises with Black Kites in parts of Africa, for example, where wintering birds from Europe, birds moving from other regions within the continent and local breeding pairs may all occur together at the same time.

In northern Europe, the onset of winter brings cold weather and, in some areas, nearly constant snow cover. In itself, this is not enough to cause a total exodus, as some birds of prey do not migrate southwards at all. It does, however, bring about a disappearance of insects, and snow cover or extremely hard weather may make mammals, especially small ones, disappear for long periods of time, which results in the emigration of many birds dependent on these prey types. Therefore, many bird predators move south in search of more favourable conditions and a more reliable supply of food.

Honey Buzzards, which feed mainly on bees, wasps and their larvae, leave their summer homes in Europe for Africa during September, and do not return again until early summer. Hobbies, too, migrate south—they feed on small birds but also depend to a large extent on flying insects. Cold weather is equally bad for the Osprey: fish are then seldom found at the surface of the water, and birds from the northern parts of the population must go south in search of better conditions. Those found much farther south are non-migratory.

Merlins from northern regions are bird-feeders, and if they are to survive in winter they must follow the small birds south. Some winter in Britain, where there is often a more localized movement of British Merlins down from the high moorland (which is virtually devoid of small birds in winter) to lower-lying or coastal areas. It is true that some kestrels in Britain follow much the same sort of pattern, but apart from a dispersion of the young birds after leaving the nest, those living in lowland areas are largely sedentary.

Among the larger species, Red Kites in continental Europe are migrants, while the relict population in central Wales is resident. Rough-legged Buzzards come south from Arctic and sub-Arctic regions in search of better supplies of the small rodents on which they feed; some

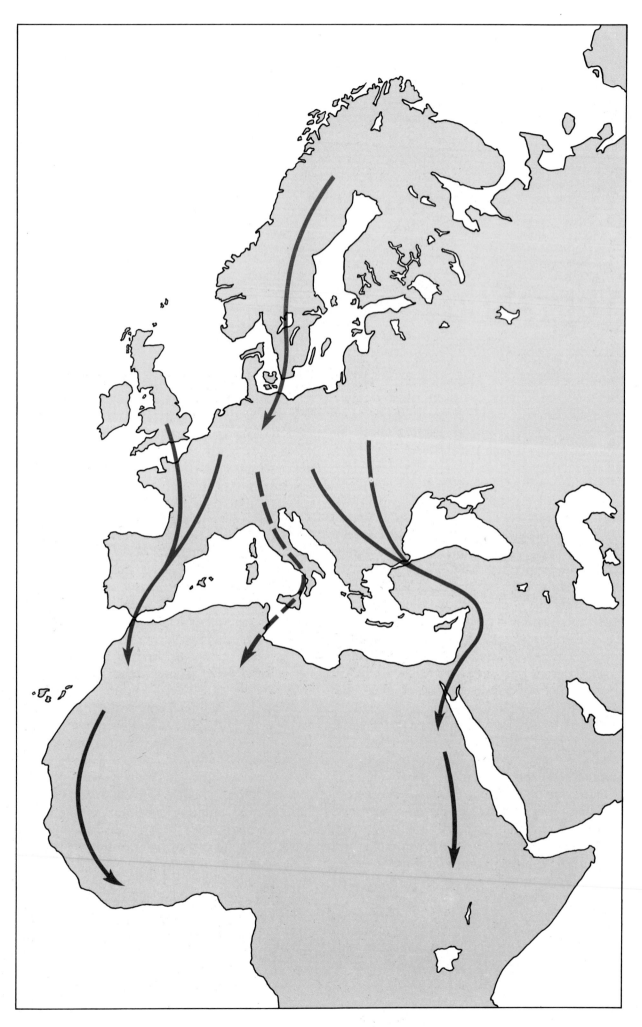

*Left : Long-winged,
soaring raptors migrate
along well-defined
routes—the major
European flyways are
shown here. Note that
most birds of prey
avoid crossing the
Mediterranean directly*

reach Britain every winter, but exceptional numbers occurred in the winters of 1973 and 1974. Northern Golden Eagles are also migratory, but those further south (including those in Scotland, some of which must endure very hard winter conditions) are resident. In the northern populations of the White-tailed Eagle we find a particularly good example of a species in which the adults are sedentary but the immature birds wander widely.

In the tropics, migratory movements are often governed by the cycle of wet and dry seasons. This is particularly true of those birds of prey which feed on small mammals and small reptiles, both of which are more easily found and caught in dry conditions when cover may be sparse. These birds will therefore nest in the dry spell when food is most abundant and move elsewhere when the rains come. In west Africa, for example, the little African Swallow-tailed Kite breeds in semi-desert country, where the insects which form its main diet are both numerous and accessible, and moves into the savannah zone once the wet season begins.

One bird of prey uses the migration of other birds to its own advantage. Many species profit from the concentrations of small migrants or even migrate with them to obtain a ready supply of prey, but Eleonora's Falcon is even further adapted to this travelling food supply. It is a migrant itself, breeding in the Mediterranean and wintering in Malagasy, but it does not lay its eggs until July or August. This means it has young in the nest just as many small

migrants are passing through the region on their way south, the latter then providing an abundant source of food.

Local movements or concentrations of raptors may result from a temporary abundance of prey in the area. Some species seem particularly sensitive in this respect, and often the timing of their breeding season coincides with a glut of food. In Europe, this is seen in 'lemming years' or during 'vole plagues' when these small rodents reach one of their cyclic population peaks, and in Africa examples of more short-lived local movements might be those which occur in response to the appearance of a horde of migrating locusts or when a grass fire drives many insects and small animals into the open. In situations like these, loose associations and even flocks of birds of prey which are normally solitary can occur. There are some species which regularly hunt in flocks while in winter quarters, a good example being Swainson's Hawk which migrates from North America south to the Argentine. Flocking is commonly seen during migration itself when birds come together through following set routes along hill ranges or where they gather at 'bottlenecks' before undertaking short sea crossings.

Many birds migrate by night, but no bird of prey does so. During their journeys they have no enemies to fear except possibly other raptors, and, as we shall see in the final chapter, man. Daylight travel is therefore generally safe. Various experiments have shown that birds appear to have an innate sense of direction, but visible landmarks are important to diurnal migrants, and to some extent immature birds migrating for the first time, often not in company with experienced adults, must acquire skill from experience.

Another aspect of daytime migration is that it takes place during the hours when thermals–rising currents of warm air–occur. These are of considerable importance to many migrant raptors as they enable the birds to travel long distances without using much energy. Unlike many small birds, raptors do not build up their fat reserves prior to migration but travel for long periods without food, or feed as they go along. For most species migration cannot be quite the hazardous and exhausting business it must be for many small birds.

Fair weather and favourable winds are prerequisites for quick and efficient migration. A sudden change of weather or wind direction can

Above: Black Kite; the European race migrates to southern Africa in the winter. The birds 'steer' in flight by subtle sideways movements of their flexible, forked tails

98

Above : The Red-tailed Hawk is typical of many soaring birds of prey which follow well-defined routes on migration, using high ground to make the maximum use of thermals while travelling and avoiding direct sea crossings

Right : Another migratory North American raptor. Swainson's Hawk winters south in Argentina. It commonly feeds in flocks or small parties in its winter quarters

move migrants off course or even force them to take an entirely wrong direction. Birds of prey, in spite of their powerful flight and ability to travel in the most fearsome winds, can be affected by freak weather conditions like other species and may turn up in the wrong place – to the delight of local birdwatchers.

The long-winged, soaring raptors migrate using well-defined routes, along mountains and hill ridges where there is a plentiful supply of thermals and upcurrents of air. They often begin a day's movement when the air is sufficiently warm to produce the first thermals, circling upwards and soaring, often to a considerable height, before gliding off to find the next thermal. In this way they can cover long distances in a day, often at a fairly high speed, making almost effortless progress, in an extension of their normal methods of travelling. Many smaller birds of prey can soar quite well, even though they may only do so irregularly or when displaying, and on migration they readily adopt the same methods used by their bigger relatives, with equal success. If you watch the great raptor passage out of Europe at the eastern end of the Mediterranean, you will find that birds soaring and gliding past include not only recognized

exponents such as the Honey Buzzard but also a number of smaller birds such as the Levant Sparrowhawk.

Besides following these well-defined inland routes, migrating birds of prey also tend to follow coastlines. Some species, such as the falcons, do fly directly across the open sea, but most, especially the big, soaring species, are reluctant to cross large expanses of water. In some parts of southern Europe it is not at all unusual to see migrating raptors moving westwards or eastwards since many of them avoid crossing the Mediterranean directly. Some certainly do so, no doubt with some 'island hopping' here and there, but the majority either cross to Africa via the Straits of Gibraltar, or go via the Bosporus and the Middle East. Because a place like the Bosporus forms a sort of bottleneck and on some autumn days is overflown by thousands of migrant hawks, it has become a Mecca for birdwatchers in recent years. Further north, many Scandinavian birds cross to mainland Europe through southern Sweden, rather than overflying the Baltic, and here Falsterbo is the most famous observation point.

A similar pattern of migration occurs in North America, where raptors migrate southwards

along the great mountain chains of the west and east, largely avoiding a direct sea-crossing and passing into South America via the narrow corridor of Central America. Many hawks which breed beyond the St Lawrence in Canada and throughout New England follow the mountain ridges to eastern Massachusetts, cross the Hudson river and pass over New Jersey until at last they are concentrated into a narrow flyway through Pennsylvania. This passes the famous Hawk Mountain, where the classic migration studies of birds of prey began. Among the thousands which pass this point from August to November are many accipiters, Broad-winged and Red-tailed Hawks, and some Bald and Golden Eagles.

Similar flight-lanes also occur in other parts of America – Cape May in New Jersey is another notable site, where Sharp-shinned Hawks from the north and Ospreys, Turkey Vultures and others from the north-east turn west to follow the coastline rather than head out across the open sea. The isthmus of Central America sees raptor migration on a scale equal to that through the Middle East; during a very short spell in October, for example, huge numbers of Swainson's and Broad-winged Hawks pour through

en route to their wintering grounds in South America.

Much less is known about movements in Asia, but there must be some really spectacular movements across such a vast continent. Some raptors from central Asia, such as Griffon Vultures and Lammergeiers, appear to cross the high Himalayas to winter in northern India, while kites breeding at fairly high altitudes in these great mountains move down to lower levels after the breeding season.

In areas south of the Equator, there is a tendency for some raptors to move northwards, although this seems uncommon among southern African and southern Australasian species. Such movements are also known among some South American raptors: the Red-tailed Buzzard and the Long-winged Harrier both have marked northerly migrations, the latter reaching as far as the Guianas. Another northward movement, but of quite a different kind, occurs in the Florida population of the Bald Eagle. The young move considerable distances north shortly after fledging; it has been suggested that this is to escape the hottest summer weather, but this curious movement remains one of the many unsolved mysteries of bird migration.

Birds of Prey Today

In this book we have looked at the diversity of birds of prey and learned about their ways of life and how they are adapted to them. They are a successful and varied group of birds, geared to a life of predation or scavenging, attracting a great deal of interest and study, even if many tropical species and some others are still largely unknown in the wild. We have also hinted at rarity, at persecution as a result of ignorance and misunderstanding, and implied the need for conservation. While it is true that in some regions—generally away from direct contact with man—raptors are often very numerous, marked decreases, gradual declines and local extinctions have occurred elsewhere. With good reason, naturalists and conservationists are very concerned for the future of a number of species.

It is already apparent that most of the problems faced by birds of prey stem from a conflict, real or imagined, with man's interests. Much of what follows deals with the more civilized parts of the world, where the problems at present seem most acute and, equally, where they are best documented. In large areas of what has become known as the 'Third World', these problems may not yet be so critical or, because observers are so few there, may have gone undetected—but it is probably reasonable to expect that trends there will not be dissimilar. Increased destruction of habitats through industrialization, urbanization, agricultural changes and land reclamation, with increasingly heavy application of pesticides to combat disease and famine, not to mention improvements in hygiene and civilization generally, could hardly make it otherwise.

Rare or endangered species are often described as being on the verge of extinction. This phrase must be used cautiously—total extinction can and does occur, and indeed threatens several raptor species currently, but more often partial or local extinction is what is meant. A species may become extinct quite naturally in the course of evolution when it can no longer find a suitable living environment. This may be because it cannot compete with a more successful species, which gradually supplants it, but this is a very long-term process which is probably not relevant to any bird of prey except the California Condor at the moment.

Over the past few centuries human intervention has undoubtedly increased the possibility of extinction for many species living in very restricted habitats or with highly specialized requirements. An example is the Guadalupe Caracara, the only raptor known to have become extinct in the last 300 years. On this dry, bare island, the Guadalupe Caracara existed in isolation from the similar Common Caracara of the mainland, in harmony with its harsh environment until man appeared on the scene. Many were shot (it was probably very tame), its young and eggs were destroyed by domestic goats and, by about 1900, it had disappeared forever.

A number of other birds of prey are restricted to islands where a long-established ecosystem is now seriously imbalanced by human interference. These are threatened by changes of habitat and land-use, by direct human persecution, by the introduction of domestic animals, or by the appearance of animals like the rat—and by other predators introduced by man to control the rat and other pests.

The Seychelles Kestrel, for example, is now very rare, due, it is thought, to a combination

of human pressure and competition with the Barn Owl–a bird introduced to the islands to control a large and troublesome population of rats, themselves aliens. Similarly, because of direct human persecution the Mauritius Kestrel is among the two or three rarest birds in the world. Probably no more than ten individuals were alive in 1974, when only one pair reared young in the wild. Controversy arose when some of the last birds were captured, in a desperate attempt to save the species from extinction by breeding in captivity. Whether this last-ditch effort will succeed remains to be seen. Sadly, the Mauritius Kestrel may have reached the point of no return.

The situation in the Philippines is just as grave for one of the most magnificent of all the world's birds of prey, the huge Philippine Monkey-eating Eagle. This big, long-lived and slow-breeding bird is threatened in several ways. The primeval forests in which it lives are gradually being cleared for agriculture; it has long been in demand for zoos–a trend which, fortunately has gone into reverse; and, of course, it has been persecuted by proponents of the erroneous theory that any big bird with a hooked beak must be classed as vermin. Over and above all

these is its prestige value among the islanders as a stuffed trophy–a threat which, like habitat destruction, has grown while the others have dwindled. It seems that only the establishment of large nature reserves, enforcement of laws concerning the capture and export of the eagles and, above all, a radical change in the attitudes of the islanders themselves can save this fine creature.

The California Condor is perhaps the most famous of all the very rare birds of prey and is certainly one which, to the credit of American conservationists and biologists, has been closely studied for many years.

This huge, primitive New World vulture is in decline as a species in evolutionary terms. It is one of the last representatives of a group of huge scavengers which, it is believed, were among the archetypal birds of prey. Perhaps its extinction was still many hundreds of years away when the nineteenth century dawned, but already its range in north-west America was contracting, and by 1900 it was probably confined to the Californian region. About 60 birds survive today in a small area of California, reduced to this number by wanton and illegal shooting and the poisoning of carcasses, and threatened by

Right : The magnificent Monkey-eating Eagle of the Philippines is threatened with extinction through the destruction of the forests in which it lives, and by trophy hunting, capture for animal dealers and direct human persecution

Above : One of the four young White-tailed Sea Eagles which figured in an unsuccessful attempt to reintroduce this species to Scotland, where it last bred 60 years ago

major human incursions. It is rigorously protected and given as much sanctuary as possible through several agencies working more or less in concert and, for the moment at least, its decline seems to have been halted. Total protection of its final refuge is by no means guaranteed for the future, however, nor is total law enforcement possible, and until both these conditions are satisfied it must remain on the list of the world's most endangered species.

The number of species threatened with total extinction is small at present, but the list of birds in decline in part of their range is much longer. If we deal with the causes chronologically we must first of all consider the question of full-scale persecution.

This has been a mainly European problem. Persecution was and still is carried out on a lesser scale in those parts of America, Africa and Australasia colonized by Europeans, even though some notable slaughter has been carried out in all those continents. It is also important to realize that civilized man has been the systematic killer: in more primitive communities control methods have always been used against raptors which kill livestock, but never in such an organized and ruthless way.

Although many European countries were persecuting birds in some numbers by the end of the eighteenth century, it was during the following century that they were slaughtered relentlessly and in unbelievably large numbers in the interest of game preservation and, to a lesser extent, livestock protection. The sheer volume of the statistics on record is staggering, so much so that it seems incredible that any birds of prey survive in Europe at all. The Dutch ornithologist, Dr Maarten Bijleveld, has related the grim tale, and a few examples of his figures illustrate the point amply.

During the nineteenth century many countries paid official bounties for the killing of raptors—indeed the system still exists in some areas. The official toll in Scandinavia was huge. In Norway alone 223,487 raptors were killed between 1846 and 1900, over 88,000 of these being Golden and White-tailed Eagles. In Britain, an enormous upsurge in game-rearing and keepering led to slaughter on a similar scale. Even the statistics for individual estates can be quite frightening—in one Scottish estate, 1,372 birds were destroyed in 3 years. The wide-scale collection of eggs and specimens was also rife, especially once the persecuted raptors became rarities.

Top left : Adult White-tailed Sea Eagle in flight. This bird is declining in its major European stronghold in Scandinavia, partly through human pressures and partly through chemical poisoning

Above and right : The huge California Condor is a primitive species, close to extinction. Today only 50 or so survive in the coastal mountains of southern California

By the early part of this century Britain had lost the Osprey and the White-tailed Sea Eagle as breeding birds as a result of human persecution. The Goshawk and the Red Kite had practically vanished long before. German figures run into thousands too, and in a short spell of full bounty payments from 1852 to 1857 the Netherlands accounted for 39,233 birds of prey–and the account goes on, country by country, until we can conclude that our nineteenth-century forbears were responsible for the destruction of literally millions of raptors.

The early part of the twentieth century saw little improvement except that tallies became smaller as bird of prey numbers decreased. If it did little else of value, the Great War at least provided a respite during which men were too busy killing one another to worry much about birds. This happened again in the Second World War, and in the last few decades the slaughter has slowed down appreciably with the increased interest in wildlife. And yet it is idle to suppose that the massacre has stopped or is even negligible. Migrating raptors are shot by the thousand for sport in the Lebanon, Malta and North Africa, for instance, and many hunters in southern Europe still kill birds of prey. Some horrifying figures reflect the scale on which the killing continues–between 1945 and 1968 Austrians

Above left: Dead Kestrel, strung up by a gamekeeper. Many birds of prey are slaughtered annually in the interests of game preservation–a killer of small rodents, the Kestrel is wholly innocent

Left: Dead hawks and owls, poisoned by persistent toxic chemical residues used in agriculture

Above : Diagram of a food chain, showing how chemical residues build up to their greatest accumulation in a bird of prey at the end of the chain

Right : A gin trap : this cruel and barbaric trap, although illegal for many years, is still widely used in Britain to 'control' birds of prey

accounted for over 393,000 raptors, and Bijleveld has estimated that in the last 15 to 20 years alone several million birds of prey have been destroyed by European hunters.

There can be no doubt at all that the blame for what can only be described as a massive decline of most raptors in Europe, and much of the senseless slaughter which caused it, lies at the door of the European sportsman. One hundred years ago their killing was done in ignorance. Today, when we know so much more about predator-prey relationships and when scientific research has established beyond any reasonable doubt that birds of prey do not exert a controlling influence on the numbers of game species, there is less excuse. Certainly ignorance persists in many areas, but now it is often reinforced by prejudice or a simple contempt for research findings–ironically in some cases, where the work has been sponsored by the game interests themselves. Dead hawks on keepers' gibbets may still be seen in some parts of Europe, and the old ways die hard. The barbarous pole-trap (a steel-jawed trap mounted on a post or pole, where hawks would often perch) has been illegal in Britain for most of this century, but a recent campaign carried out by the

Royal Society for the Protection of Birds showed that it is still widely used.

In Western Europe the climate of opinion is changing, albeit slowly, and more and more sportsmen are becoming aware of the mistakes of the past and are adopting a more enlightened attitude. For many of them the term 'vermin' is on the way out and many are becoming interested and involved in conservation.

While the killing of birds of prey to protect livestock has been carried out throughout history on a small scale, it has usually been perpetrated out of ignorance, misunderstanding or wishful thinking. It would be quite wrong to deny that some raptors kill poultry or take lambs, for example, but the damage they do is usually much exaggerated and is often better prevented by simply improving stock protection or changing the practice of land-use than by shooting or poisoning the offending birds.

The vexed question of eagles and lambs illustrates the situation well. The Golden Eagle will occasionally take a young lamb, it is true, but by far the bulk of those it eats are found as carrion: no reliable evidence exists to show that it has ever had a disastrous effect on sheep populations anywhere, and yet in parts of Scotland it is still persecuted remorselessly, year after year. In parts of the western United States it has been relentlessly hunted and killed for alleged damage to stock, and not only in the traditional ways – light aircraft carrying marksmen with rifles are used. The Wedge-tailed Eagle in Australia has gained even more notoriety as a lamb-killer than the Golden Eagle and has probably been persecuted more heavily than any other big eagle anywhere in the world, even though it is no more guilty than is the Golden Eagle in this respect.

Newer, but equally insidious factors have also been at work in recent decades, with no less disastrous results. One of these is the ever-increasing destruction of habitat through the clearance of woodlands or forests, or, conversely, through afforestation, reclamation, drainage of wetlands, and industrial and urban expansion. Any of these could have a marked effect on specialized birds of prey such as the Snail Kites or Marsh Harriers needing certain limited conditions for breeding. Some species on the other hand may adapt to change – Kestrels take quite readily to life in urban or industrial surroundings – and a few may even benefit from it. Sparrowhawks and Hen Harriers, for instance, have certainly prospered in those parts of Britain where commercial forests are now growing.

For some species, it is not habitat but food supply which changes or disappears. Better standards of hygiene and improved agricultural practices have certainly been a factor in the decline of vultures in some parts of Europe. Similar trends in the future could affect their abundance in other parts of the world.

Another recent, catastrophic development is the pollution of raptors' food supplies by highly toxic, persistent residues of certain chemical substances used as pesticides. The most notorious of these have been the chlorinated hydrocarbons, of which DDT is the best known, but mercury compounds are also widely used. Still more recently evidence has come to light of pollution by the polychlorinated biphenols (PCBs), especially in marine environments where they occur as dumped industrial waste.

In the continuing battle to check disease, both in human and domestic animals, and to combat agricultural pests, these toxic chemicals have undoubtedly had spectacular successes. Unfortunately, their persistence was not forseen (many of them take years to break down) and their side-effects were not fully investigated or understood. It was left to the naturalists of the United States and Western Europe to discover that their

Right : A highly specialized bird like the Snail Kite could suffer from the loss of the wetland habitats it frequents. It has already become a rarity in the United States

Below : Although persecuted, the Hen Harrier has become much more widespread in the new, man-made habitats provided by young conifer plantations

accumulating residues were having disastrous effects on wild animals and birds. A crop which has been treated with a highly toxic insecticide such as DDT will be fed upon by many insects. The crops and the insects feeding on them form the first two links in what is called a food chain; the next link is formed by an insect-eating bird which may consume the insects in large quantities, especially if sub-lethal doses have made them easier to catch than usual. The bird will thus ingest all the residues present in the insects it eats—which may be enough in some cases to cause marked effects even before the end of the chain is reached. The last link in the food chain is the bird-eating hawk which may eat several insectivorous birds, and in whose tissues the chemical residues will achieve even higher concentrations. The hawk, at the end of the food chain, may thus become highly contaminated and suffer quite disastrous side-effects from a well-intentioned attempt to control insect pests which harm crops.

These side-effects appear in several forms. At the highest levels of contamination the bird is simply poisoned so badly that it dies, often in convulsions. Lower levels of contamination can be equally serious: birds lay infertile eggs or eggs with thin, fragile shells or they may become so unbalanced that their normal breeding behaviour is affected, resulting in them not brooding their eggs properly, breaking them in the nest, or even eating them. While a widespread decrease in numbers of birds of prey was suddenly apparent in both the United States and Europe, it was probably reduced breeding success or total breeding failure in some species that was most obvious and which gave naturalists the greatest cause for alarm.

Ornithologists in two continents were quick to take action. Important research studies were soon undertaken in Britain (and in other Western European countries soon afterwards) and in the United States. For once, the rising tide of public opinion, often running ahead of the publication of research results which confirmed its worst fears, began to achieve the right sort of publicity and, after a long struggle, even the right sort of remedial action. Little by little, governments were persuaded to ban certain chemicals or to impose restrictions on their use: already in areas where the use of chlorinated hydrocarbons has been banned, or restricted, the breeding performance of the raptors most at risk has slowly improved.

A great deal remains to be done, of course, and the fact that the very substances being phased out in Europe and America are being widely used in other parts of the world causes grave concern. The battle against the highly poisonous mercury compounds and the PCBs has scarcely begun, although some progress has been made. In fairness to the chemical manufacturers, who not unnaturally opposed the naturalists' claims at the outset, it must be said that once the facts were known many of them were quick to lend their considerable resources to programmes of research and recovery and to speed up the development of safer, less persistent pesticides as replacements.

The ornithological literature of the last 15 years is thick with records of declining numbers, reductions in breeding success and contamination levels in eggs, dead birds and chicks. Even birds breeding in non-contaminated areas were found to have residues picked up on migration or in winter quarters. Notable examples include the catastrophic decline in breeding success among Ospreys in the eastern United States, a similar phenomenon among nesting Golden Eagles in parts of western Scotland, the almost complete disappearance of Sparrowhawks from south-east England and, most cataclysmic of all, the widespread population crash of the Peregrine in almost all areas where studies have been carried out.

The Peregrine seems to have been the worst hit of all the raptors and the history of its decline has probably been followed more closely and is better documented than that of any other species. It is such a magnificent bird that its endangered position has caused great concern among nature-lovers, and it is also regarded as one of the most delicate 'natural barometers' we possess, so that its population fluctuations can indicate the state of the whole environment. With an almost worldwide distribution it has always been regarded as one of the most successful of all raptors in evolutionary terms. As a bird-feeder which takes a wide range of prey it is characteristically at the top of a food chain and as such very liable to contamination. Its numbers had decreased in many parts of Europe and North America before the era of toxic chemicals, often through persecution, and yet it was still flourishing at a reduced level of population. Given freedom from persecution there was no reason to suppose the Peregrine would become an endangered species.

Toxic chemicals have changed this situation radically, and there are now real fears that before long it may vanish from mainland Europe altogether. In Norway its population is now tiny, while in Sweden it has dropped from a few hundred about 30 years ago to only a dozen pairs; Finland's population is now only 6 pairs and Denmark's 10 pairs have been reduced to one, Belgium's 20 to none, West Germany's 400 to 70, Poland's 200 to perhaps 20, Czechoslovakia's 50 to 10, Switzerland's 60 to 5 and Austria's 20 to less than 5. In France only about 100 Peregrines remain, and hopes for Italy's 20 or so pairs are slender, although there may still be as many as 150 in Sardinia and 80 in Sicily. Numbers in Spain seem to have remained high, however, and the species seems to be surviving quite well there. The British population was around 700 pairs in 1945, but a survey in 1963 showed that less than half the territories of these birds were occupied, while, even more alarmingly, only 16 per cent of them produced any young. By 1971 an improvement was noticed, with a further 10 per cent of the territories occupied and 25 per cent of them producing young. The situation in Britain is unique in that its Peregrine population is the only one, in Europe or the United States, to have started to recover from its marked decline.

The situation for the Peregrine in North America is also serious. While it is practically impossible to estimate the large Arctic and northern populations accurately, in the west, and perhaps also in the maritime states of the northeast, a marked and continuing decline has occurred in areas where comparisons with past information can be made. The position in the eastern states is one of total extinction during the last 15 to 20 years. In 1964 all the known 133 nest-sites were visited and not a single adult bird was seen. Toxic chemicals had abruptly finished what other forms of human disturbance and persecution had begun. The toxic chemical saga is a particularly sad one and, with the equally tragic catalogue of slaughter already described, is one of the two major features of the current decline of raptors in many parts of the civilized world.

Lesser–though far-reaching–factors are also contributing to the decline. Egg-collecting is no longer the scourge it used to be, but it still goes on to a greater extent than is often realized, and it is a much more serious problem than any of its practitioners will ever admit. The collection of specimens, either by amateurs or museums is now much reduced, but zoos, wild-life parks and private collectors are responsible for the capture of many live birds of prey. While it is very sad to see an eagle or a great vulture confined to a cage, unable to soar in the skies and in most cases unable to breed, a case can be made for the educational function of collections which the public can see, and in very limited circumstances for direct conservation and breeding of very rare species. It is unfortunate, however, that some well-known collections only pay lip-service to these ideals and display animals merely to make money. The more reputable zoos take trouble to provide their birds with a better environment and are scrupulous in obtaining specimens, especially if these are rare or endangered. Unfortunately the middle-men who procure and sell birds of prey are often quite uninterested in the sources of the birds or their ultimate destinations, or whether the transactions involved are strictly legal or not. The traffic in birds of prey, especially from some parts of Asia, is a lucrative business, often carried out with no thought at all to the welfare of the birds in transit. The problems of import and export are now a matter of international concern.

Another reason birds of prey are captured alive is falconry, an ancient and honourable sport with its origins in Asia and the Middle but with many devotees today in Europe, America and elsewhere. The true falconer is a dedicated man able to devote the major part of his time to his birds. Their well-being is his chief concern and the real aficionado would rather have no birds at all than do the job half-heartedly or endanger the existence of a species in the wild through his desire to take birds. Whether one approves of the ethics of falconry or not, it is not to be denied that falconers have contributed significantly to our knowledge of raptors and that today the best of them have become some of the leading allies of conservationists.

Unfortunately, the true falconers are in the minority: more common are men who are only able to man their birds in their spare time, who show scant regard for the principles of conservation or for the laws protecting birds of prey and who are less than scrupulous about obtaining their birds from the wild. Worse still, some of them have reduced falconry to a money-making enterprise with exhibition-flying and other sorts of gimmickry, popularizing the sport without regard to the consequences. Falconry is not for the masses: it is a highly specialized art and those who have either the time or the resources to practise it will always be few in number.

Left : Two falconer's birds—a Bat Falcon (far left) and a Prairie Falcon

Above: Pakistani falconers with their birds. The ancient sport of falconry had its origins in the East, where it is still widely practised, and has a wide following in Europe and North America

At present birds of prey, especially those in Europe and parts of North America, face numerous man-made problems which may easily result in their disappearance. The questions which remain to be answered are how these man-made problems may be resolved and what has been done so far? Fortunately, the popularity of raptors among naturalists and conservationists has ensured that a great deal has happened – but it must be admitted that even more effort is required, and the lessons learned in two continents could well be of the utmost importance in other parts of the world in the years to come.

Laws protecting birds of prey, and close restrictions on their capture, importation and exportation, are essential. The ultimate aim must be complete protection for all species, but with machinery for exceptions to be made as necessary. Achieving these ideals is in practice a slow, difficult process. In Europe, for example, full protection for all bird of prey species has so far been achieved in only nine countries. Elsewhere there is only partial protection in law, or none at all. Overall, the position is far from satisfactory; more laws concerning importation, for instance, are certainly needed. There are,

of course, many complications: enforcing a law may be nearly impossible, as conservationists in France or parts of the United States would readily attest and, as the small but active group in Italy have found to their cost, a huge and powerful hunting lobby can exert so much political pressure that workable bird protection legislation may sometimes seem like an absurd dream.

World opinion, at least in Europe and the English-speaking world, is beginning to recognize the dangers of exploiting rare birds and animals for money or to satisfy the passing whims of fashion. Birds of any sort have not often been in the limelight, but in the long term they benefit from the campaigns to save whales, tigers and other animals, so much so that several countries have already introduced strict import and export controls for birds, including the birds of prey.

Protection is of course very important. In Europe especially, the establishment of nature reserves or other protected zones where all wildlife can live unmolested is crucial. Many such areas are already in existence, but many more are needed, especially in the southern and eastern parts of the continent. The United States

has long been in the vanguard in setting up reserves, sanctuaries and national parks; some of the recently independent African states are actively protecting their great wildlife heritage, and in Australia and New Zealand the movements towards active conservation are rapidly gaining momentum. A start has been made in various parts of Asia, and in Russia and some of her satellite countries considerable programmes have been in force for some years. Setting up reserves is not a solution in itself, however; proper management based on detailed research is essential if they are to be maintained, and there must also be some form of public participation.

The special schemes established to protect individual pairs of local populations of birds of prey are too numerous to mention, but their number grows annually. Just how well they can be made to work is amply demonstrated by 'Operation Osprey', run by the Royal Society for the Protection of Birds in Scotland. What began as an exercise in protecting an extremely rare bird has become a major factor in gaining public sympathy and support, without which conservation cannot work. Over 100,000 people have come to see these birds annually in recent years, and other schemes in Europe have used this one as their model.

Various other schemes are in operation already and might well be expanded. French and Spanish ornithologists, for instance, have begun some interesting experiments in providing food (mainly waste from slaughterhouses) for vultures

Above: Lammergeier and Choughs. This huge vulture has all but disappeared from Europe, but is the subject of artificial feeding experiments in Spain and may be reintroduced in the Alps

returning to Scotland after an absence of 50 years is a notable exception. It might, for example, be possible to reinstate the Peregrine in the eastern United States by this means. Attempts have already been made to reintroduce the White-tailed Sea Eagle to Britain (unsuccessfully so far), Goshawks are being moved in some parts of Europe, and an attempt is to be made to re-establish the Lammergeier in the Alps. It cannot be stressed too often that these experiments require considerable thought and expertise. Carrying them out in a general way on a large scale, as has often been advocated, could do more harm than good.

Recent attempts to breed birds of prey in captivity, specifically for release to the wild, have become fashionable. No doubt it could be of great value, especially to falconers in an era when permits to take birds in the wild are difficult to obtain. The whole business is beset with problems, not the least of which is getting the birds to breed in the first place: relatively few species have done so to date. One of the few schemes so far which is particularly well founded and of considerable value is that by which American workers are trying to rear and release Peregrines: it is pleasing to record that some successes were achieved in 1974.

Above all else there lies the need to educate people in the ways of birds of prey, for only by gaining their understanding can all the excesses caused by ignorance and intolerance be brought to an end. In short, we must find more ways of convincing people that a hawk is every bit as desirable, useful and beautiful as a song-bird or a game-bird. This means more research to back up the broad principles we understand already, but also effective dissemination of the results of this research: learned papers in obscure journals are most desirable, but if they are read only by ornithologists how can we expect farmers, gamekeepers, sportsmen and the public to know about them and, more important, to understand and believe them? Like the careless bird-watcher or photographer, or the narrow-minded protectionist, the scientist can so easily become the bird of prey's worst enemy if he does not appreciate that the birds belong to everybody.

There is happily an ever increasing interest in the world's wildlife, coupled with the desire to understand more about it and to help it when, often through no fault of nature, it is in trouble – so we may hope that, with a better understanding of their ways of life, our magnificent and beautiful birds of prey will survive for our children's grandchildren to enjoy.

in the Pyrenees, while in Germany and the United States some successful work has been carried out in moving eggs from one nest to another (sometimes even involving two different species) where breeding success with the original parents seemed unlikely. Such 'artificial' tactics are often condemned by purists who maintain that nature should be left to take its own course, but in a world where man has caused so much damage it is reasonable that he should use some of his ingenuity to redress the balance – as long as the facts are known first and the work is in competent and responsible hands.

Similar arguments apply to the controversial attempts to reintroduce birds of prey to areas where man has caused their extinction. Few birds of prey return naturally, although the Osprey

Species List

The following list includes all the members of the Order Falconiformes. The scientific names and sequence follow that adopted by Brown and Amadon in the standard work, *Eagles, Hawks and Falcons of the World*. English names differ from those used by these authorities in one or two cases.

The Order Falconiformes is sub-divided into three Sub-orders, each of which is further sub-divided into families. Within families, closely related birds are grouped together in genera (singular genus). The genus name is the first of the two scientific names and *both* scientific names form the species name.

Sub-Order Cathartae

Family Cathartidae

Cathartes aura	Turkey Vulture
Cathartes burrovianus	Yellow-headed Vulture
Cathartes melambrotus	Greater Yellow-headed Vulture
Coragyps atratus	Black Vulture
Sarcorhamphus papa	King Vulture
Gymnogyps californianus	California Condor
Vultur gryphus	Andean Condor

Sub-Order Accipitres

Family Pandionidae

Pandion haliaetus	Osprey

Family Accipitridae

Aviceda cuculoides	African Cuckoo-falcon
Aviceda madagascariensis	Madagascar Cuckoo-falcon
Aviceda jerdoni	Jerdon's Baza
Aviceda subcristata	Crested Baza
Aviceda leuphotes	Black Baza
Leptodon cayanensis	Grey-headed or Cayenne Kite
Chondrohierax uncinatus	Hook-billed Kite
Henicopernis longicauda	Long-tailed Honey Buzzard
Henicopernis infuscata	Black Honey Buzzard
Pernis apivorus	Honey Buzzard
Pernis celebensis	Barred Honey Buzzard
Elanoides forficatus	Swallow-tailed Kite
Machaerhamphus alcinus	Bat Hawk
Gampsonyx swainsonii	Pearl Kite
Elanus leucurus	White-tailed Kite
Elanus caeruleus	Black-winged Kite, Black-shouldered Kite
Elanus notatus	Australian Black-shouldered Kite
Elanus scriptus	Letter-winged Kite
Chelictinia riocourii	African Swallow-tailed Kite
Rostrhamus sociabilis	Snail or Everglade Kite
Rostrhamus hamatus	Slender-billed Kite
Harpagus bidentatus	Double-toothed Kite
Harpagus diodon	Rufous-thighed Kite
Ictinia plumbea	Plumbeous Kite
Ictinia misisippiensis	Mississippi Kite
Lophoictinia isura	Square-tailed Kite
Hamirostra melanosternon	Black-breasted Buzzard Kite

Milvus migrans	Black, Common or Pariah Kite	*Eutriorchis astur*	Madagascar Serpent Eagle
Milvus milvus	Red Kite		
		Polyboroides typus	African Harrier Hawk, Gymnogene
Haliastur sphenurus	Whistling Hawk, Whistling Eagle		
Haliastur indus	Brahminy Kite	*Polyboroides radiatus*	Madagascar Harrier Hawk
Haliaeetus leucogaster	White-bellied Sea Eagle	*Geranospiza caerulescens*	Crane Hawk
Haliaeetus sanfordi	Sanford's Sea Eagle		
Haliaeetus vocifer	African Fish Eagle	*Circus assimilis*	Spotted Harrier
Haliaeetus vociferoides	Madagascar Fish Eagle	*Circus aeruginosus*	Marsh Harrier, Swamp Hawk
Haliaeetus leucoryphus	Pallas' Sea Eagle	*Circus ranivorus*	African Marsh Harrier
Haliaeetus leucocephalus	Bald or American Eagle	*Circus maurus*	Black Harrier
Haliaeetus albicilla	White-tailed Sea Eagle, Erne	*Circus cyaneus*	Hen Harrier, Marsh Hawk
Haliaeetus pelagicus	Steller's Sea Eagle	*Circus cinereus*	Cinereous Harrier
		Circus macrourus	Pallid Harrier
Ichthyophaga nana	Lesser Fishing Eagle	*Circus pygargus*	Montagu's Harrier
Ichthyophaga ichthyaetus	Grey-headed Fishing Eagle	*Circus melanoleucus*	Pied Harrier
		Circus buffoni	Long-winged Harrier
Gypohierax angolensis	Palm Nut Vulture, Vulturine Fish Eagle		
		Melierax metabates	Dark Chanting Goshawk
Neophron percnopterus	Egyptian Vulture	*Melierax canorus*	Pale Chanting Goshawk
		Melierax gabar	Gabar Goshawk
Gypaetus barbatus	Lammergeier, Bearded Vulture		
		Megatriorchis doriae	Doria's Goshawk
Necrosyrtes monachus	Hooded Vulture		
		Erythrotriorchis radiatus	Red Goshawk
Gyps bengalensis	Indian White-backed Vulture		
Gyps africanus	African White-backed Vulture	*Accipiter gentilis*	Northern Goshawk
Gyps indicus	Indian Griffon, Long-billed Vulture	*Accipiter henstii*	Henst's Goshawk
		Accipiter melanoleucus	Black or Great Sparrowhawk
Gyps rueppellii	Rüppell's Griffon	*Accipiter meyerianus*	Meyer's Goshawk
Gyps himalayensis	Himalayan Griffon	*Accipiter buergersi*	Bürger's Sparrowhawk
Gyps fulvus	Griffon Vulture	*Accipiter ovampensis*	Ovampo Sparrowhawk
Gyps coprotheres	Cape Vulture	*Accipiter madagascariensis*	Madagascar Sparrowhawk
		Accipiter gularis	Japanese Lesser Sparrowhawk
Torgos tracheliotus	Lappet-faced Vulture	*Accipiter virgatus*	Besra Sparrowhawk
		Accipiter nanus	Celebes Little Sparrowhawk
Sarcogyps calvus	Indian Black or King Vulture	*Accipiter rhodogaster*	Vinous-breasted Sparrowhawk
		Accipiter erythrauchen	Moluccan Sparrowhawk
Aegypius monachus	European Black or Cinereous Vulture	*Accipiter cirrhocephalus*	Collared Sparrowhawk
		Accipiter brachyurus	New Britain Sparrowhawk
		Accipiter nisus	European Sparrowhawk
Trigonoceps occipitalis	White-headed Vulture	*Accipiter rufiventris*	Rufous-breasted Sparrowhawk
		Accipiter striatus	Sharp-shinned Hawk
Circaetus gallicus (including *C. g. pectoralis* and *C. g. beaudouini*)	Sort-toed or Serpent Eagle, Black-breasted Harrier Eagle, Beaudouin's Harrier Eagle	*Accipiter erythropus*	Red-thighed Sparrowhawk
		Accipiter minullus	African Little Sparrowhawk
		Accipiter castanilius	Chestnut-bellied Sparrowhawk
Circaetus cinereus	Brown Harrier or Snake Eagle	*Accipiter tachiro*	African Goshawk
Circaetus fasciolatus	Southern Banded Snake Eagle	*Accipiter trivirgatus*	Crested Goshawk
Circaetus cinerascens	Smaller Banded Snake Eagle	*Accipiter griseiceps*	Celebes Crested Goshawk
		Accipiter trinotatus	Spot-tailed Accipiter
Terathopius ecaudatus	Bateleur	*Accipiter luteoschistaceus*	Blue and Grey Sparrowhawk
		Accipiter fasciatus	Australian Goshawk
Spilornis holospilus	Philippine Serpent Eagle	*Accipiter henicogrammus*	Gray's Goshawk
Spilornis rufipectus	Celebes Serpent Eagle	*Accipiter novaehollandiae*	White, Grey or Vinous-chested Goshawk
Spilornis cheela	Crested Serpent Eagle		
Spilornis klossi	Nicobar Serpent Eagle	*Accipiter griseogularis*	Grey-throated Goshawk
Spilornis elgini	Andaman Serpent Eagle	*Accipiter melanochlamys*	Black-mantled Accipiter
		Accipiter imitator	Imitator Sparrowhawk
Dryotriorchis spectabilis	Congo Serpent Eagle	*Accipiter albogularis*	Pied Goshawk
		Accipiter haplochrous	New Caledonia Sparrowhawk
		Accipiter rufitorques	Fiji Goshawk

Accipiter poliocephalus	New Guinea Grey-headed Goshawk	*Buteo albicaudatus*	White-tailed Hawk
Accipiter princeps	New Britain Grey-headed Goshawk	*Buteo polyosoma*	Red-backed Buzzard
		Buteo poecilochrous	Gurney's Buzzard
Accipiter soloensis	Grey Frog Hawk	*Buteo albonotatus*	Zone-tailed Hawk
Accipiter brevipes	Levant Sparrowhawk	*Buteo solitarius*	Hawaiian Hawk
Accipiter badius	Shikra	*Buteo ventralis*	Red-tailed Buzzard
Accipiter butleri	Nicobar Shikra	*Buteo jamaicensis*	Red-tailed Hawk
Accipiter francesii	France's Sparrowhawk	*Buteo buteo*	Common Buzzard
Accipiter collaris	American Collared Sparrowhawk	*Buteo oreophilus*	African Mountain Buzzard
Accipiter superciliosus	Tiny Sparrowhawk	*Buteo brachypterus*	Madagascar Buzzard
Accipiter gundlachi	Gundlach's Hawk	*Buteo lagopus*	Rough-legged Buzzard
Accipiter cooperii	Cooper's Hawk	*Buteo rufinus*	Long-legged Buzzard
Accipiter bicolor	Bicoloured Sparrowhawk	*Buteo hemilasius*	Upland Buzzard
Accipiter poliogaster	Grey-bellied Goshawk	*Buteo regalis*	Ferruginous Hawk
		Buteo auguralis	African Red-tailed Buzzard
Urotriorchis macrourus	African Long-tailed Hawk	*Buteo rufofuscus*	Jackal or Augur Buzzard
Butastur rufipennis	Grasshopper Buzzard Eagle	*Morphnus guianensis*	Guiana Crested Eagle
Butastur liventer	Rufous-winged Buzzard Eagle		
Butastur teesa	White-eyed Buzzard	*Harpia harpyja*	Harpy Eagle
Butastur indicus	Grey-faced Buzzard Eagle		
		Harpyopsis novaeguineae	New Guinea Harpy Eagle
Kaupifalco monogrammicus	Lizard Buzzard		
		Pithecophaga jefferyi	Philippine Monkey-eating Eagle
Leucopternis schistacea	Slate-coloured Hawk		
Leucopternis plumbea	Plumbeous Hawk	*Ictinaetus malayensis*	Indian Black Eagle
Leucopternis princeps	Prince's or Barred Hawk		
Leucopternis melanops	Black-faced Hawk	*Aquila pomarina*	Lesser Spotted Eagle
Leucopternis kuhli	White-browed Hawk	*Aquila clanga*	Spotted Eagle
Leucopternis lacernulata	White-necked Hawk	*Aquila rapax*	Tawny or Steppe Eagle
Leucopternis semiplumbea	Semiplumbeous Hawk	*Aquila heliaca*	Imperial Eagle
Leucopternis albicollis	White Hawk	*Aquila wahlbergi*	Wahlberg's Eagle
Leucopternis occidentalis	Grey-backed Hawk	*Aquila gurneyi*	Gurney's Eagle
Leucopternis polionota	Mantled Hawk	*Aquila chrysaetos*	Golden Eagle
		Aquila audax	Wedge-tailed Eagle
Buteogallus anthracinus	Common Black Hawk	*Aquila verreauxi*	Verreaux's or Black Eagle
Buteogallus aequinoctialis	Rufous Crab Hawk		
Buteogallus urubitinga	Great Black Hawk	*Hieraaetus fasciatus*	Bonelli's Eagle, African Hawk-eagle
Harpyhaliaetus solitarius	Black Solitary Eagle	*Hieraaetus pennatus*	Booted Eagle
Harpyhaliaetus coronatus	Crowned Solitary Eagle	*Hieraaetus morphnoides*	Little Eagle
		Hieraaetus dubius	Ayres' Hawk-eagle
Heterospizias meridionalis	Savannah Hawk	*Hieraaetus kienerii*	Chestnut-bellied Hawk-eagle
Busarellus nigricollis	Fishing Buzzard	*Spizastur melanoleucus*	Black and White Hawk-eagle
Geranoaetus melanoleucus	Grey Eagle-buzzard	*Lophoaetus occipitalis*	Long-crested Eagle
Parabuteo unicinctus	Bay-winged or Harris's Hawk	*Spizaetus africanus*	Cassin's Hawk-eagle
		Spizaetus cirrhatus	Crested or Changeable Hawk-eagle
Buteo nitidus	Grey Hawk, Mexican Goshawk, Shining Buzzard-hawk	*Spizaetus nipalensis*	Mountain or Feather-toed Hawk-eagle
Buteo magnirostris	Roadside, Insect, Large-billed or Tropical Broad-winged Hawk	*Spizaetus bartelsi*	Java Hawk-eagle
		Spizaetus lanceolatus	Celebes Hawk-eagle
Buteo leucorrhous	Rufous-thighed Hawk	*Spizaetus philippensis*	Philippine Hawk-eagle
Buteo ridgwayi	Ridgway's Hawk	*Spizaetus alboniger*	Blyth's Hawk-eagle
Buteo lineatus	Red-shouldered Hawk	*Spizaetus nanus*	Wallace's Hawk-eagle
Buteo platypterus	Broad-winged Hawk	*Spizaetus tyrannus*	Black Hawk-eagle
Buteo brachyurus	Short-tailed Hawk	*Spizaetus ornatus*	Ornate Hawk-eagle
Buteo swainsonii	Swainson's Hawk		
Buteo galapagoensis	Galapagos Hawk	*Stephanoaetus coronatus*	Crowned Eagle

Oroaetus isidori	Isidor's Eagle	*Microhierax latifrons*	Bornean Falconet
		Microhierax erythrogonys	Philippine Falconet
Polemaetus bellicosus	Martial Eagle	*Microhierax melanoleucus*	Pied Falconet

Family Sagittariidae

Sagittarius serpentarius — Secretary Bird

Sub-Order Falcones

Family Falconidae

Daptrius ater	Yellow-throated Caracara
Daptrius americanus	Red-throated Caracara
Phalcoboenus carunculatus	Carunculated Caracara
Phalcoboenus megalopterus	Mountain Caracara
Phalcoboenus albogularis	Darwin's or White-throated Caracara
Phalcoboenus australis	Forster's Caracara, Johnny Rook
Polyborus lutosus	Guadalupe Caracara *(extinct)*
Polyborus plancus	Common Caracara
Milvago chimango	Chimango
Milvago chimachima	Yellow-headed Caracara
Herpetotheres cachinnans	Laughing Falcon
Micrastur ruficollis	Barred Forest Falcon
Micrastur plumbeus	Sclater's Forest Falcon
Micrastur mirandollei	Slaty-backed Forest Falcon
Micrastur semitorquatus	Collared Forest Falcon
Micrastur buckleyi	Traylor's Forest Falcon
Spiziaptery circumcinctus	Spot-winged Falconet
Polihierax semitorquatus	African Pigmy Falcon
Polihierax insignis	Fielden's Falconet
Microhierax caerulescens	Red-legged Falconet
Microhierax fringillarius	Black-legged Falconet

Falco naumanni	Lesser Kestrel
Falco rupicoloides	Greater or White-eyed Kestrel
Falco alopex	Fox Kestrel
Falco sparverius	American Kestrel or Sparrowhawk
Falco tinnunculus	Common Kestrel
Falco newtoni	Madagascar or Aldabra Kestrel
Falco punctatus	Mauritius Kestrel
Falco araea	Seychelles Kestrel
Falco moluccensis	Moluccan Kestrel
Falco cenchroides	Australian or Nankeen Kestrel
Falco ardosiaceus	Grey Kestrel
Falco dickinsoni	Dickinson's Kestrel
Falco zoniventris	Madagascar Banded Kestrel
Falco vespertinus	Red-footed Falcon
Falco chicquera	Red-headed Falcon, Red-headed Merlin
Falco columbarius	Merlin, Pigeon Hawk
Falco berigora	Brown Hawk
Falco novaezeelandiae	New Zealand Falcon
Falco subbuteo	European Hobby
Falco cuvieri	African Hobby
Falco severus	Oriental Hobby
Falco longipennis	Little Falcon, Australian Hobby
Falco eleanorae	Eleonora's Falcon
Falco concolor	Sooty Falcon
Falco rufigularis	Bat Falcon
Falco femoralis	Aplomado Falcon
Falco hypoleucos	Grey Falcon
Falco subniger	Black Falcon
Falco biarmicus	Lanner Falcon
Falco mexicanus	Prairie Falcon
Falco jugger	Laggar Falcon
Falco cherrug	Saker Falcon
Falco rusticolus	Gyrfalcon
Falco deiroleucus	Orange-breasted Falcon
Falco fasciinucha	Taita Falcon
Falco kreyenborgi	Kleinschmidt's Falcon
Falco peregrinus	Peregrine Falcon

Bibliography

The literature on birds of prey is enormous, though much of it appears in scientific journals or is otherwise difficult for the general reader to obtain. The following are mostly recent and are recommended for further reading:

BENT, Arthur Cleveland, *Life Histories of North American Birds of Prey*, 2 volumes, Dover Publications, New York 1958.

BIJLEVELD, Maarten, *Birds of Prey in Europe*, Macmillan, London 1974.

BROWN, Leslie, *African Birds of Prey*, Collins, Glasgow 1971; Houghton Mifflin, Boston 1971.

BROWN, Leslie, *Eagles*, Barker, London 1970; Arco, New York 1970.

BROWN, Leslie and AMADON, Dean, *Eagles, Hawks and Falcons of the World*, Hamlyn, Feltham, Middlesex 1969.

GROSSMAN, Mary and HAMLET, John, *Birds of Prey of the World*, Cassell, London 1965; Potter, New York 1970.

Studies of single species are few, but the following are recommended:

GORDON, Seton, *The Golden Eagle*, Collins, Glasgow 1955.

KOFORD, C. B., *The California Condor*, National Audubon Society and Dover Publications, New York 1953.

TUBBS, Colin, *The Buzzard*, David and Charles, Newton Abbot, Devon 1974.

Most bird handbooks give good concise accounts for the regions they cover, but for identification the following field guides are particularly useful:

BOND, James, *Birds of the West Indies*, Collins, Glasgow 1960.

FALLA, R. A., SIBSON, R. and TURBO, E., *Field Guide to the Birds of New Zealand*, Collins, Glasgow 1966.

PETERSON, G. M. and HOLLOM, P., *Field Guide to Birds of Britain and Europe*, Collins, Glasgow 1974.

PETERSON, Roger T., *Field Guide to the Birds*, Houghton Mifflin, Boston 1968.

PETERSON, Roger T., *Field Guide to the Western Birds*, Houghton Mifflin, Boston 1972.

PROZESKY, O. P. N., *Field Guide to the Birds of Southern Africa*, Collins, Glasgow 1971.

WILLIAMS, J. G., *Field Guide to the Birds of East and Central Africa*, Collins, Glasgow 1972.

A wholly new concept in bird of prey identification is to be found in:

PORTER, R. F., *Flight Identification of European Raptors*, T. and A. D. Poyser, Berkhamstead, Hertfordshire 1974.

Index

Note: Every member of the Order Falconiformes is included in the Species List on page 122.